The Tudors

THE KINGS AND QUEENS OF ENGLAND'S GOLDEN AGE

Jane Bingham

This edition published in 2012 by Arcturus Publishing Limited
26/27 Bickels Yard, 151–153 Bermondsey Street,
London SE1 3HA

AD002442EN

Printed in the UK

Contents

Chapter 1
Fighting for the Crown 7

Chapter 2
A Dynasty is Born – the Reign of Henry VII 33

Chapter 3
The Promise of Greatness – Young Henry VIII 87

Chapter 4
**Turmoil and Tyranny – the Later Reign of
   Henry VIII** 125

Chapter 5
**The Boy King and the Nine Days' Queen –
   Edward and Jane** 175

Chapter 6
Bloody Mary – the Life and Reign of Mary I 223

Chapter 7
**The Making of a Great Queen – Young
   Elizabeth** 273

Chapter 8
The End of the Dynasty – Gloriana 327

Epilogue
What Was the Tudors' Legacy? 379

Chapter 1
FIGHTING FOR THE CROWN

The battlefield at Bosworth was scattered with the bodies of the wounded, dead and dying. For almost three hours, the armies of York and Lancaster had fought tenaciously, but now the bloody struggle was over. And in the midst of the carnage lay King Richard III, the last English monarch to die in battle.

Richard had worn his crown proudly into battle, and as he lay dying – so the chroniclers said – it had rolled away under a hawthorn bush. When the fighting was done, the muddy crown was rescued and placed on the head of the young victor. It was a crucial moment in English history. As Henry Tudor accepted the English crown, the Wars of the Roses came to an end and the Tudor era began.

The dynasty that Henry Tudor founded would rule for more than a hundred years, presiding over a golden age of music, art and literature. Under the Tudors, England experienced peace and prosperity, transforming itself from an obscure northern kingdom into a major player in European politics. But who was Henry Tudor and how did he come to claim the English throne?

The Wars of the Roses – Fighting for the Crown

Between the years 1455 and 1485 a bitter power struggle was waged between two branches of the Plantagenet dynasty of the English royal family, each branch descended from King Edward III. On one side were the descendants of the Duke of Lancaster, whose supporters wore a red rose emblem. On the other were the offspring of the Duke of York, who sported a white rose. Over a turbulent period of thirty years the English people were ruled by one Lancastrian king – Henry VI – and three Yorkist rulers – Edward IV, Edward V and Richard III. The last major clash of the Wars of the Roses took place on 22 August 1485 at Bosworth Field, close to the town of Bosworth in what is now Leicestershire, when Henry Tudor, heir to the House of Lancaster, defeated the Yorkist king, Richard III.

A Royal House Divided – Lancasters and Yorks

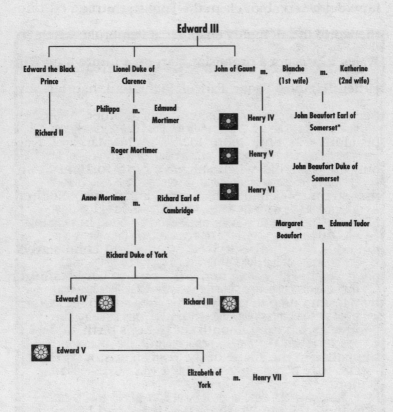

Key:

 Red rose – House of Lancaster

White rose – House of York

* Illegitimate since born out of wedlock (before John of Gaunt married Katherine).

Who Was Henry Tudor?

On 28 January 1457, a puny baby boy struggled into the world in a draughty chamber at Pembroke Castle in Wales. It was not a promising start for a future king. His father, Edmund Tudor, Earl of Richmond, had already been dead three months, and his mother, Margaret Beaufort, was little more than a child. Margaret was only 14 years old when she gave birth to Henry, and the strain of childbirth nearly killed her. Neither Margaret nor Henry was expected to live, but against the odds they both survived. Mother and child stayed on at Pembroke Castle under the care of Lord Stafford, who lost no time in marrying his own son to the young widow. Within three months of Henry's birth, he had a stepfather, in the shape of the English aristocrat Henry Stafford.

In their remote Welsh castle, Henry and his mother were far removed from the English court, but they could not remain unaffected by the turmoil waging there. The Wars of the Roses had begun two years before Henry's birth as a result of Richard Duke of York's claims to the English throne, and one of the struggle's early victims was Henry's father. Edmund Tudor had been fighting for the House of Lancaster in 1456 when he was captured by Yorkist supporters and thrown into prison. In the dungeons of Carmarthen Castle in Wales, Edmund contracted plague and died. His son must have grown up listening to horror stories of these bloody wars and their bitter legacy.

Henry Tudor's links with the House of Lancaster were strong, albeit tinged with scandal (see panel opposite). Both his parents could claim royal ancestry, and his uncle and grandfather, Jasper and Owen Tudor, were passionate supporters of the Lancastrian cause. But his position close to the House of Lancaster was fraught with danger. By the time of Henry Tudor's birth, power was slipping from the grasp of the reigning Lancastrian monarch, King Henry VI, and none of the king's relatives was safe from potential harm. As a junior member of the House of Lancaster, young Henry Tudor was destined to be a valuable pawn in some highly dangerous political games.

Henry's Royal Ancestry – Loose Connections

More than a whiff of scandal clung to Henry Tudor's royal connections. His mother, Margaret, was directly descended from John Beaufort, the illegitimate child of John of Gaunt, Duke of Lancaster, and third surviving son of King Edward III. On his father's side, Henry's grandfather, Owen Tudor, had been clerk of the wardrobe to Katherine of Valois, wife of King Henry V. Owen's position involved keeping the queen's domestic accounts, and in the course of his job he developed a close friendship with his royal mistress. After the king's early death, Owen secretly married Katherine and fathered four children with her, including Henry's father, Edmund, who were half-brothers and sisters to King Henry VI. Such questionable connections were not to be flaunted, and even after he had won the English crown, Henry Tudor never stressed his claim to the throne.

A Troubled Childhood

Henry's first experience of adult power games came when he was just 4 years old. In 1461, his closest male relatives – his uncle Jasper and grandfather Owen Tudor – engaged in a life-and-death struggle to defend their king, leading the Lancastrian forces at the Battle of Mortimer's Cross, a site near Wigmore in Herefordshire. Their army was soundly defeated, and the Lancastrian King Henry VI was replaced by the Yorkist King Edward IV. Once securely in power, the Yorkists lost no time in executing Owen Tudor, although his son Jasper managed to escape, travelling first to Scotland and then to France.

With his grandfather dead, and his uncle in exile, the 4-year-old Henry was left without a guardian and protector. But another dominant figure quickly took over this role. As one of the leading Yorkist nobles in Wales, Sir William Herbert was in a very powerful position, and he seized the chance to take control of a potentially valuable young ward. Henry was welcomed into the Herbert family home in Raglan Castle, south-east Wales, and a new era in his childhood began. The move marked the start of a long period of separation from his mother for Henry, as Margaret moved to England with her husband, Henry Stafford.

Apparently the Herbert family treated young Henry well. He was allowed to keep his title, Earl of Richmond (inherited from his father), and was provided with a good education. There was even talk of Henry marrying Herbert's daughter, but this peaceful way of life was not to last. In 1469, when Henry was 12 years old, Sir William Herbert was defeated at the Battle of Edgecote Moor, and was later executed by the all-powerful Earl of Warwick (popularly known as the 'Kingmaker'). In the following year, the Lancastrian monarch, Henry VI, was restored to the throne and Jasper Tudor returned from exile to take over the role of guardian of his young nephew. At the age of 13, Henry Tudor was presented at the English royal court, where he began a new life as a favoured relative of the king.

All Change

The months that followed must have been a confusing time for young Henry. Bereft of his erstwhile guardian and young companions, he was forced to forget his Yorkist adopted family and put his Welsh childhood firmly behind him as he was catapulted into a world of English power politics. But Henry Tudor's change of fortune was once again short-lived. Within twelve months of his return to the throne, King Henry VI had been thrown into prison. On 4 May 1471 the Yorkists won a decisive victory at the Battle of Tewkesbury, and in the course of the fighting Henry's only son and heir, Edward, was killed. Less than three weeks later, King Henry died in the Tower of London (murder was widely suspected) and the Yorkist leader, King Edward IV, returned to the throne. This dramatic turnaround in the fortunes of the House of Lancaster put England securely back in the hands of the Yorkists. It also meant that Henry was the new Lancastrian heir – and in mortal danger from the House of York.

Jasper Tudor lost no time in ferrying his nephew to safety across the English Channel – much to King Edward's displeasure. In the words of a contemporary Tudor historian, the Italian Polydore Vergil, the king reacted 'very grievously' to the news that 'the only imp now left of Henry VI's brood' had escaped his clutches, and offered a generous reward to anyone who could bring the fugitives back to England. But fortunately for Henry, Jasper had found a powerful protector for his nephew. Duke Francis II of Brittany was an independent-minded ruler who refused to be browbeaten by an English king. Ignoring all inducements to hand over his charge, he issued a statement that he would provide protection for Jasper and Henry, so long as they undertook not to lead an attack against King Edward.

Henry in Exile

Henry Tudor remained in exile for fourteen years. During his long stay at the Breton court, he must have often gazed longingly across the English Channel. But

Murder in the Tower – Who Was To Blame?

Less than a month after the death of King Edward IV, on 9 April 1483, his eldest son, Edward V, was sent to the Tower of London, where he was joined on 16 June by his younger brother, Richard of Gloucester. At first the two princes were spotted in the courtyard of the Tower, but by the end of summer they had disappeared. The fate of the two Yorkist heirs remains unknown, and it is presumed that they were murdered. But the question remains – who was responsible for their deaths?

Most historians have accused King Richard III of the ruthless murder of his nephews, but others have suggested some intriguing alternative scenarios. Some see the Duke of Buckingham, a close ally of Richard in the early months of his reign, as a likely suspect. A few have suggested that it was Henry Tudor who orchestrated the crime, as a way of removing some significant obstacles to his own claim to the throne.

England under Edward IV was a very dangerous place for a Lancastrian heir. Following his return to the throne in 1471, King Edward had established a strong power base, and with the birth of his two sons, the Yorkist succession seemed invincible. By the time Henry reached his 26th year, he must have resigned himself to a lifetime of semi-captivity. Then everything changed in a few momentous months.

In the spring of 1483, King Edward IV caught a cold. A few weeks later he was dead, at the age of 40. At the time of his death, his eldest son, also called Edward, was just 12 years old, so Edward's uncle, Richard of Gloucester, was proclaimed Lord Protector of the Realm. Richard's role was to rule on behalf of the boy king, Edward V, until he was mature enough to assume power in his own right. But within a few months, Edward and his younger brother Richard had been incarcerated in the Tower of London, never to be seen again. The imprisonment and subsequent disappearance of the two princes in the Tower is one of the most notorious incidents in English history – and one that is still debated today. But even before their presumed murder, in an attempt to consolidate his hold on power Richard had had the two young princes declared illegitimate, and himself crowned King Richard III.

King Richard and His Enemies

The reign of King Richard III is one of the most controversial in English history. To 16th-century writers Sir Thomas More and William Shakespeare, Richard Crookback was a deformed villain, perpetrator of foul deeds. Later historians have attempted to rehabilitate his reputation, stressing his popularity among the people of northern England. Some have absolved him of responsibility for the fate of the two princes; Buckingham, once a close ally of Richard's, is viewed as a more likely suspect. Whatever Richard's qualities as a ruler, he had little chance to display them. During his short reign, he faced determined opposition from some of the most powerful families in the kingdom.

Chief among Richard's enemies was Elizabeth Woodville, widow of Edward IV and mother of the two Yorkist princes.A formidable matriarch, she was described at the time as the most beautiful woman in England and was also widely believed to be a witch. Elizabeth devoted herself to wreaking revenge on Richard and regaining power for her family, and she seized the chance to achieve her ends by forming an alliance with the Tudors – and especially with Margaret Beaufort.

Henry's mother Margaret was probably the only woman in England who could prove a match for Elizabeth Woodville. Driven by a burning ambition for herself and her son, she had married one of the country's leading magnates following the death of her second husband. Margaret's third husband, Lord Thomas Stanley, held the position of Constable of England under King Richard III, but he was prepared to lend his support to whichever ruler could offer him most power. Now, with her powerful husband's help, Margaret planned to set her exiled son on the English throne.

Plots and Promises

By the late summer of 1483, Elizabeth and Margaret had hatched a plan to place their children in power. Elizabeth and her allies would lend their support to Henry Tudor in his bid to gain the English crown if Henry would promise to marry Princess Elizabeth, daughter of Elizabeth and Edward IV. The scheme had some evident advantages. By uniting the rival Houses of Lancaster and York, Henry would gain maximum support for his invasion, and a marriage between the two royal houses would help to secure Henry's claim to the throne.

Henry's first attempt at invasion took place in October 1483. His supporters had prepared for a multi-pronged attack, with Henry's fleet landing on the coast of Wales just as several uprisings were set in motion in various English towns. In the event, however, their plans were foiled by poor communications and terrible weather. King Richard acted swiftly to punish the rebels, and several of them had to flee for their lives to join Henry in

Brittany. Finding himself at the heart of a growing court in exile, Henry decided to hold a solemn ceremony of intent. On Christmas Day 1483, in Rennes Cathedral, the young pretender to the throne proclaimed himself King Henry VII of England, accepted his supporters' oaths of allegiance, and promised to marry Princess Elizabeth as soon as he had secured the crown. It was Henry's first kingly act, and an important step towards the union of the rival families that had fought for the crown for thirty years.

Timely Escape and New Plans

Before Henry Tudor could achieve his goal, he had to deal with another threat to his life. In the summer of 1484, Henry's protector, the elderly Duke Francis of Brittany, fell seriously ill, leaving his kingdom in the care of advisers. Taking advantage of the situation, King Richard III put pressure on the Breton counsellors to surrender Henry Tudor to the English crown. The royal request was granted, but, fortunately for Henry, Bishop

Morton of Ely managed to send a warning message to him. Henry made a rapid escape eastward into northern France, riding on horseback disguised as a page, with his enemies hot in pursuit only an hour behind him.

Once he was safely settled in Paris, Henry began to gather a group of loyal supporters, including John De Vere, Earl of Oxford, a seasoned battle commander, and several men who would later serve him as ministers. King Charles VIII of France, fearful of Richard III's foreign ambitions, also offered assistance in the form of a loan of 60,000 francs and 1,800 mercenaries. One French account described the mercenaries as 'the most unruly men that could be found', but Henry was grateful for any help that he could get. He had learned that Richard was trying to entice some of his supporters back to the Yorkist cause, and so he knew that he needed to act quickly and decisively. On 1 August 1485 Henry's tiny fleet of just six ships left the port of Harfleur in northern France, and sailed out into the English Channel heading for the coast of Wales.

Invasion!

The voyage from France to Wales took a week – plenty of time for Henry to contemplate the task that lay ahead. His army consisted of around 500 English supporters, as well as the company of French mercenaries, making up a total of just over 2,000 men. To add to this tiny army, Henry hoped to enlist the support of the Welsh lords, and his main hope lay with his stepfather, Lord Thomas Stanley, and Thomas's powerful brother, Sir William Stanley. However, Henry was only too aware that none of these allies could be relied upon. Meanwhile, King Richard had gathered a well-disciplined force and was lying in wait for Henry at Nottingham.

Just before sunset on 7 August 1485, the Tudor fleet reached Milford Haven, a port on the south-western tip of the Welsh coast. Henry greeted the land of his birth, kneeling humbly to sing the psalm *'Judica me, Deus, et discerne causam meam'* ('Judge me, O God, and plead my cause') before mustering his troops. His army first marched northwards along the Cardiganshire coast before turning inland to cross the Cambrian Mountains and follow the River Severn into England. Five days into the march, Henry gained his first ally: the powerful landholder Rhys ap Thomas with his company of Welsh warriors. Four days later, a local lord, Gilbert Talbot, brought another 500 fighting men.

At Tamworth, in Leicestershire, Henry held a secret meeting with Thomas and William Stanley, but neither of the brothers would commit to his cause. King Richard had taken Lord Thomas' eldest son hostage as a guarantee of his father's loyalty. Meanwhile, Sir William was hedging his bets, and waiting to see which way the battle would swing. Henry knew that his army would be outnumbered by almost two to one, but he had no choice but to march towards Leicester, where Richard's forces were stationed.

During the course of 21 August, the opposing armies advanced towards each other until, by nightfall, they were within firing distance. Sir William Stanley remained in a position of neutral observer, establishing his camp on a nearby hill with a clear view of both forces. Not far off, his brother Lord Thomas Stanley was also waiting with his troops to see how the fighting developed. In the dangerous game of war, Thomas Stanley was playing for very high stakes. If he made a move against King Richard, his own son's life was in danger, but he was also charged by his powerful wife with the task of championing his stepson Henry. As the brothers watched and waited to make their move, everything was poised for the battle the following day.

The Battle of Bosworth Field

The two men preparing to lead their troops into battle were very different characters. At the age of 32, King Richard was a seasoned general and leader of men. When he was just 18, he had played a crucial part in the battles that restored his brother Edward to the throne, and during Edward's reign, he demonstrated his loyalty and skill as a military commander. In reward for his loyalty, he had been appointed as Governor of the North, becoming the most powerful noble in England. As an administrator, he had proved himself to be efficient, fair and just, and in the city of York, where he was based, he was regarded with much love and affection. Contrary to later popular myths, King Richard almost certainly had no physical deformities, and he was certainly skilled and brave in battle. In short, he was a formidable opponent for Henry.

Henry Tudor's claims to leadership in battle were much less well-founded than Richard's. During his years in France he had trained in the arts of war, but his skills had never been tested in battle. And neither had he ever been a leader of fighting men. Having spent his entire adulthood as an exile in a foreign court, Henry could only rely on the support of a tiny handful of English nobles, while even his claim to the throne was not entirely convincing.

While just four years separated the opponents, their past experience was worlds apart, and, in terms of leadership, all the advantages seemed to lie with

Richard. Even numbers of troops were in the king's favour: it is estimated that at the start of battle, Richard commanded around 8,000 men while Henry had 5,000. All Henry's hopes for victory rested on the shoulders of the two ambitious brothers waiting and watching from the top of the nearby hill.

By 6 am on the morning of 22 August, Henry's army was on the move, marching slowly towards the hill where Richard's forces were encamped. The king was waiting for the Stanley brothers to offer their support, but when he signalled for them to advance, William made no response, while Thomas flatly refused, heading off instead in Henry's direction. When the Earl of Northumberland also failed to take action, Richard decided to lead the charge himself. Riding straight for Henry, he fought defiantly, killing first Henry's standard-bearer and then another guard before launching an attack on Henry himself.

It was a crucial moment in the battle, when the death of either leader would have decided the fate of

Shakespeare's Henry Tudor – Bringer of Peace and Plenty

William Shakespeare's play *King Richard the Third* ends on the battlefield at Bosworth with the death of Richard and the crowning of Henry Tudor. In Henry's final prophetic speech, he looks forward to a golden time of peace and plenty under his Tudor heirs.

'England hath long been mad, and scarred herself;
The brother blindly shed the brother's blood;
The father rashly slaughtered his own son;
The son, compelled, been butcher to the sire;
All that divided York and Lancaster,

United in their dire division.
O, now let Richmond and Elizabeth,
The true succeeders of each royal house,
By God's fair ordinance conjoin together,
And let their heirs, God, if his will be so,
Enrich the time to come with smooth-faced peace,
With smiling plenty, and fair prosperous days.'
(Act 5, Scene 5)

their country, but fate intervened in the form of Lord Thomas Stanley's men, who encircled the king and forced him to retreat. died soon afterwards in the heat of the battle, and the news spread rapidly that the king was slain.

With the death of Richard III, Sir William Stanley finally joined the battle on Henry's side, driving the remnants of Richard's army southwards. Close to a hummock of ground later named Crown Hill, Henry's men acclaimed him as their new king, and, according to legend, Lord Thomas Stanley set Richard's crown on Henry Tudor's head. Richard's body was symbolically humiliated, stripped naked and led away slung across the back of a horse. Henry proceeded to London and his coronation as the first Tudor king of England.

Chapter 2
A DYNASTY IS BORN – THE REIGN OF HENRY VII

For the young Henry VII, the Battle of Bosworth Field was just the beginning. At the age of 28, he faced the daunting task of hanging on to the throne and passing it on to his heirs – something that every English king since Henry V had failed to do. In a land of which he knew little, surrounded by enemies, he was expected to bring peace and stability. Thirty years of civil war had delivered a dangerous degree of power into the hands of the English barons. The royal coffers were empty, and England's reputation among its foreign rivals stood perilously low. The kingdom was in desperate need of healing and the English people looked to their new king to perform the miracle.

Securing the Throne

At first sight, there was little in Henry's background to prepare him for his role as king. Separated from his mother at the age of 4, he had been brought up in exile in Wales and France without a father to guide him. When he was just 12 years old, he had lost a trusted guardian (in the person of Lord Herbert) and he had been compelled to spend his early manhood in enforced idleness in the Breton court. While all the English nobles were accustomed to ruling great estates, Henry Tudor had never even run a small manor. Of his 28 years, less than two had been spent on English soil and he had no real power base in his new kingdom.

Yet despite all his evident disadvantages, Henry's troubled youth had furnished him with several useful qualities. From an early age, he had observed the power games played by others, acquiring an intimate understanding of the dangerous world of politics. Outside his small circle of trusted friends and advisers, Henry had learned not to rely on the judgements of others. Instead, he had grown accustomed to judging characters and situations for himself, only taking action after careful consideration. Above all, Henry's years of insecurity had left him with an overwhelming desire for stability – a longing that would lead to his establishment of a secure and well-funded monarchy.

Humiliating King Richard

'The body of King Richard being found among the slain, covered with wounds, dust, and blood, after suffering many shameful indignities, was hung over a horse, like a calf... The corpse was perfectly naked, the feet hung on one side, the hands on the other, and the head lately adorned with a crown, dangling like a thrum-mop. No King ever made so degraded a spectacle; humanity and decency ought not to have suffered it. Carte says they tied a rope about his neck, which is very probable, and perhaps about his feet, or he could not well have been fastened to the horse. This was meant as a disgrace to Richard, but it reflected more upon Henry, or his followers; for to insult weakness is highly blamable, but more to insult the dead.

'The corpse was exposed two days to public view, in the town hall; this was Henry's policy, to prevent a future impostor, and his pride to shew himself a conqueror, and then interred without ceremony, in the Gray-friers' church. Here Richard rested about fifty years, with a scrubby alabaster monument erected over him by Henry. At the destruction of religious houses, his remains

> *were turned out of their little tenement by the town's people, and lost, and his coffin of stone, was converted into a watering trough at the White-Horse, in Gallow-tree-gate. Thus all the grandeur for which Richard exerted uncommon talents, ended in a stile below a beggar.'*

Extract from W. Hutton's *The Battle of Bosworth Field, between Richard the Third and Henry Earl of Richmond*, published in 1813.

Henry faced pressing problems in the days and weeks following his victory at Bosworth Field. Firstly, there was the question of Richard's supporters. Should they be harshly punished? Or could they be expected to respond to reasonable treatment and swear allegiance to their new king? Henry decided on a course that tempered firmness with mercy. One of his first actions was to place the mutilated corpse of King Richard on public display – a gesture that seems shockingly brutal to modern eyes, but one which had a practical purpose. By proving conclusively that Richard was dead, Henry quashed any rumours that the former king had escaped alive, thus eliminating a potentially dangerous source of future rebellion.

Henry also dealt swiftly with a potential threat to his crown. Richard's 10-year-old nephew, Edward, Earl of Warwick, was the official heir of Richard III, and a possible figurehead for Yorkist uprisings. Within three days of his victory, Henry had sent troops to Yorkshire with orders to capture Edward. From there the boy was transported to the Tower of London, where he was housed in comfort while also being kept securely under lock and key. To the other major claimant to the throne Henry adopted a very different approach. Before his death, Richard III had named his nephew, John de la Pole, Earl of Lincoln, as his heir, but Lincoln and his father, the Duke of Suffolk, had both pledged their loyalty to Henry after Bosworth. Henry decided that, at least for the time being, he should accept the fealty of these powerful men, and Lincoln was even invited to join the Royal Council.

Immediate punishments were meted out to some

of Richard's supporters. The leading Yorkist, William Catesby, was beheaded at Leicester, three days after the battle, and the Earls of Surrey and Northumberland were imprisoned. Others had their lands confiscated – a highly effective measure with a useful bonus: it generated extra revenue for the crown. On the whole, however, Henry showed remarkable leniency in his dealings with the Yorkists. On 11 October 1485 a general royal pardon was issued to all supporters of King Richard who had not been captured. The edict displayed the new king's magnanimity, but also showed his grasp of an unavoidable fact. The Yorkists included some of the most powerful men in England, and Henry desperately needed their support if he was ever to succeed in the task of governing his kingdom.

After the chaos of war, Henry had to meet the urgent challenge of maintaining a stable government. With fewer than a hundred loyal supporters, he recognized the need to work with Richard's officials to ensure a smooth transition of power. As a general rule, any civil servant who had not played an active part on Bosworth Field was kept in place, and the royal household, the exchequer and the courts of law were run by the same functionaries as they had been in Richard's time. Naturally, some of Henry's closest supporters were given high-status posts. John Morton was made Archbishop of Canterbury and Lord Chancellor. Henry's uncle Jasper became the Duke of Bedford and was made a member of the Royal Council, while the Stanley brothers (whose grudging support at Bosworth Field had proved so vital to Henry's victory) both became royal councillors. For John de Vere, the Earl of Oxford, who had played a key role in the Tudor invasion, Henry reserved the role of High Admiral of England, Constable of the Tower and Keeper of the Royal Menagerie, a glorious collection of exotic beasts, including several leopards and lions.

One major problem confronted Henry in the days following his victory. How could he – with his questionable links to the House of Lancaster – justify his claim to the English throne? In his approach to

Mother's Boy?

Even though his mother, Margaret Beaufort, had played little part in his upbringing, the adult King Henry was devoted to her. And Margaret made the most of her royal role. At court she insisted on being referred to as 'My Lady the King's Mother', signing herself 'Margaret R'. She also refused to accept a status lower than her daughter-in-law, always wearing robes of the same quality as those of the queen, and following just one pace behind her. It has been suggested that Margaret was also responsible for ousting Elizabeth Woodville, the queen's mother, from court. History does not record how the queen felt about Margaret Beaufort, but it is not too hard to imagine Elizabeth's reactions to her mother-in-law.

this issue, as in many others during his reign, Henry displayed a remarkable grasp of realpolitik. Rather than protest the strength of his blood links to the throne (a game in which he could easily have been outplayed by the young Earl of Warwick), Henry chose instead to emphasize his role as an agent of God's will. Thanks to heavenly providence, Henry's lawyers claimed, the new king had delivered the English people from the tyranny of Richard of York. These lawyers also took care to date Henry's claim to the throne to 21 August 1485, the day before the Battle of Bosworth Field – a cunning legal tactic that transformed Henry Tudor from usurper to royal defender and rendered all Richard's supporters traitors to the crown.

On 30 October 1485, Henry Tudor was crowned king of England in Westminster Abbey. It was Henry's first public appearance as king and he took great care to impress his subjects, dressing in all the finery and jewels that he could assemble. One week later, Parliament granted the riches of the crown to Henry and his heirs. The timing of these events was entirely deliberate: Henry was determined that it could never be said that Parliament made him king. Finally, with his role as monarch firmly established, Henry turned to the other ceremony that would secure his place on the English throne – his marriage to Princess Elizabeth of York.

The Red Rose and the White

Ever since he had taken his solemn vow in Rennes Cathedral, Henry had been determined to marry Elizabeth. As the daughter of King Edward IV, she commanded the loyalty of all Yorkist supporters, and, by taking the princess as his wife, Henry hoped to turn his former enemies into allies. In an age when all royal marriages carried a weight of political significance, the union of Henry and Elizabeth was to prove crucial to their nation's fate. The marriage took place on 18 January 1486 and it marked the end of a conflict that had torn the country apart for thirty years. By this simple act of union, the red rose of Lancaster and the white rose of York were united and a powerful new symbol was born – the double red and white rose of the Tudors.

In September 1486, Elizabeth gave birth to a son at Winchester, the ancient capital of King Arthur's legendary kingdom. The royal baby was named Arthur in a deliberate move to link the Tudor dynasty to England's ancient hero. All England's nobility gathered at Winchester for the royal christening, and it seemed that God was smiling on the new king. Within a year of his coronation, Henry had not only secured his throne. He had also produced an heir, who, through his name and birthplace, forged links with Britain's distant past, as well as providing hope for a glorious Tudor future.

Early Trouble: a Yorkist Uprising

With the coming of spring in 1486, Henry decided it was time to journey in state through his realm. There were worrying rumours of pockets of rebellion, especially in the north of England, and the king resolved to assert his authority through a royal progress. Such a progress was the best way of conveying a sovereign's power and wealth to his subjects (and one that would be used to great effect by the later Tudors). And so, in April, the new English king set off for the north, accompanied by an impressive royal retinue.

Henry must have felt some anxiety as he journeyed to his northern capital of York. Less than twelve months earlier, the city had been the power base for King Richard's campaign and had been plunged into 'grete hevynesse' by Richard's death. But, in fact, trouble came from the south. Since the Battle of Bosworth Field, some of Richard's most loyal supporters had sought sanctuary in the city of Colchester in Essex. (In the 15th century, major towns and cities could provide protection for key figures so long as they promised to remain peaceably within the city walls.) With Henry away in northern England, three leading Yorkist nobles – Francis, Viscount Lovell and Humphrey and Thomas Stafford – saw their chance to break sanctuary and rise up in rebellion. Lovell travelled north, planning to ambush the king, while the Stafford brothers headed west to Worcester to stir up unrest.

An Ointment to Kill the King

One of the strangest incidents among the many conspiracies against King Henry VII concerned a pot of supposedly magic ointment. The ointment was designed to kill the king from a distance and was made by a Spanish astrologer for Sir John Kendal, one of Henry's sworn enemies. According to its creator, the mixture was to be smeared on the frame of a doorway through which the king would pass, and would immediately strike him dead. However, it was never put to the test. The messenger charged with the task of carrying the ointment to Sir John was overcome with curiosity, and decided to open the pot himself. Disgusted by the potion's appalling stench, he hastily disposed of it down a privy!

Henry was in Lincoln when he heard the news, but he refused to be deflected from his course, simply sending an armed force to confront the rebels. All those who had planned to join in the uprising were offered a simple choice: pardon and reconciliation if they agreed not to fight, or excommunication and death if they persisted with their resistance. Faced with these stark alternatives, the rebels rapidly dispersed. The Stafford brothers were imprisoned in the Tower on charges of treason against the king. Humphrey protested vehemently, claiming that his right to sanctuary had been violated, but he was overruled and executed. His younger brother Thomas was seen as a lesser threat and was later pardoned and released. For the rest of his life, Thomas Stafford was a loyal subject, but Francis Lovell was not so easily contained. He somehow managed to escape to Flanders, where he would later be involved in another plot against his king.

Lambert Simnel: Pretender to the Throne

The uprising of spring 1486 proved to be a prelude to two far more serious rebellions, each focused on the claims of a pretender to the throne. The first of these began in Oxford in the autumn of 1486, when a priest and scholar named Richard Symonds dreamed that he was tutor to a future king. The most likely candidate for the royal role was Lambert Simnel, the 10-year-old son of an organ-grinder, who proved conveniently willing to play the part of young pretender. Simnel was smuggled across the water to Ireland, where he was acclaimed as Edward, Earl of Warwick, nephew of the late King Richard III. The Irish were staunch supporters of the Yorkist cause and they readily welcomed Simnel as the rightful king of England.

In fact, the real Earl of Warwick was safely under lock and key in the Tower of London. In February 1487, when rumours of the pretender began to spread, King Henry paraded the 12-year-old earl in front of some of the most powerful people in the land. Henry must have believed that such incontrovertible proof would effectively quash any rebellion, but his plan backfired. One of the nobles who had questioned young Edward was his cousin, John de la Pole, the Earl of Lincoln, Richard III's chosen heir. Lincoln had been chafing at his loss of power ever since the Battle of Bosworth

Field, and now he saw his chance to seize the throne. Safe in the knowledge that Lambert Simnel was a fraud, Lincoln decided to throw in his lot with rebels. When the time was right, Lincoln must have reasoned, he could easily expose the young impostor and step into his shoes as the rightful claimant to the throne. With this plan in place, Lincoln crossed the English Channel, heading for the court of his powerful aunt, Margaret, Duchess of Burgundy.

The Mystery of Minster Lovell

After the Battle of Stoke Field, Francis, Viscount Lovell, was never seen again, but there were rumours that he went into hiding in his home at Minster Lovell Hall in Oxfordshire. According to a local legend, Lovell became trapped in his hiding place and starved to death, a story that was apparently confirmed when a skeleton was discovered in an underground chamber at the hall in 1708.

Within a matter of months, the Yorkists were ready for action. Lincoln was joined in Burgundy by a group of English nobles, including Francis Lovell, and in May the rebels sailed for Ireland with a force of 2,000 German soldiers. Simnel was crowned King Edward VI in Dublin, using a coronet borrowed from a statue of the Virgin Mary, before being carried through the streets of Dublin on the shoulders of the tallest man in town. With their dubious figurehead in place, the rebels prepared to launch an invasion of England.

Henry recognized that it was time for decisive action. Believing that the initial threat would come from Lincoln's powerbase in East Anglia, he marched first to Norfolk, but, meeting no opposition, soon turned west again and settled on Kenilworth, in Warwickshire, as a base for his troops. Meanwhile, Lincoln had landed in Lancashire and was leading his army across the Pennines to York, where he was confident of finding support. However, the mood in the city had changed since the time of Bosworth Field, as the city's merchants had grown used to the peace and prosperity offered by King Henry, and the rebel army was compelled to head south instead.

On 16 June 1487 the two armies met just outside Newark, at East Stoke, in a battle for the English crown. Henry's forces outnumbered Lincoln's by around 12,000 to 8,000, but the rebels had more experience, and the professionalism of the German soldiers, coupled with the wild courage of the Irishmen, gave them an early advantage on the battlefield. As the day wore on, however, the superior numbers of the Royalists began to tell, and after three hours of fighting the rebels were surrounded and defeated. Lincoln was killed in battle, along with the leaders of the German and Irish forces, and around 4,000 rebel troops. (Henry lost around 3,000 men.) Francis Lovell fled from the battlefield and was last seen urging his horse to swim across a river to safety. Lambert Simnel was captured and sent to work in the royal kitchens.

Six years later, King Henry seized the chance to

confront a group of Irish lords with their former king. When the lords gathered to dine at the royal palace, Henry made sure that Simnel served the wine. 'My masters of Ireland,' he is reputed to have said, 'you will crown apes next.'

Perkin Warbeck: the French Pretender

In the autumn of 1491, a strikingly handsome youth arrived from France in the Irish port of Cork. He was the 17-year-old Perkin Warbeck, a French-born apprentice in the weaving trade, working for a Breton cloth merchant. Warbeck was widely admired as he wandered around the town, dressed in his master's finest wares, and it was not long before the rumours began to spread. Could the handsome stranger be Prince Richard of York, second son of Edward IV, and one of the princes locked up in the Tower who were supposed dead? Those who were keen to rise up against King Henry willingly embraced this fantasy, explaining away Warbeck's evident lack of English with the story that the young Prince Richard had somehow managed to escape to France where he grew up speaking French.

Today, many historians believe that Perkin Warbeck was a deliberate plant by Yorkist conspirators. But, whatever the origin of the pretence, it soon assumed a curious reality. King Charles VIII of France welcomed Warbeck at his court and by the summer of 1492 around 100 Yorkists had travelled to join him in Paris. Two years later, the newly elected Holy Roman Emperor, Maximilian, also recognized the youth as Richard IV. Back in England, support for the impostor was growing fast, and Henry took drastic measures to nip the rebellion in the bud, confiscating the lands of several of the leading nobles who opposed him. Chief among the disloyal aristocrats was Henry's step-uncle Sir William Stanley, who held the post of chamberlain of the king's household. Confronted by disloyalty in one so close to him, Henry acted decisively, ordering Stanley's execution, but he must have felt both hurt and shaken by this betrayal.

In July 1495, Warbeck attempted a landing at Deal in Kent. His plan had been to rally support and then march on London, but his small army was routed before their leader had even disembarked. Forced to retreat, Warbeck sailed for Ireland, where he besieged the royal town of Waterford without success, before moving on to Scotland. The Scots were ancient enemies of the English and here at last Warbeck received the welcome he had expected. It is not known whether the 22-year-old King James IV of Scotland was truly taken in by Warbeck's claims, but he granted the young impostor a monthly pension and even offered him the hand of his cousin in marriage. King James also proposed to help Warbeck mount his invasion of England, and in September 1496 they launched a joint attack on the English borders.

In the event, the invasion rapidly degenerated into a brutal border raid. No public backing for 'Richard' materialized in Northumberland, and the Scottish troops seized the chance for a bonanza of looting, burning and killing. This shameful episode marked the end of good relations between the Scottish king and Perkin Warbeck, as James recognized that Warbeck would never prove an effective ally, while Warbeck took to lecturing the king about the barbarism of his troops.

In July 1497 Warbeck sailed for Ireland. Landing at Cork, he discovered he had lost his supporters there, and soon realized that he must leave Ireland or risk imprisonment. This time he headed for Cornwall, where there had recently been a rebellion against King Henry's taxes. Hoping to capitalize on the Cornishmen's discontent, Warbeck boldly promised that once he was crowned king, he would put a stop to all extortionate taxes. He was declared 'Richard IV' on Bodmin Moor. With a force of some 3,000 men, Warbeck marched on Exeter and Taunton, but in both places his army was repulsed. Meanwhile, the news reached Warbeck that King Henry had ordered one of his leading generals to lead an attack on the Cornish rebels. When Warbeck heard that the king's scouts were in Glastonbury, he panicked and fled for sanctuary, deserting his army. In

Beaulieu Abbey in Hampshire, Warbeck threw himself on the king's mercy, making a full confession of his attempt to impersonate a royal prince.

King Henry's response to Warbeck's confession was surprisingly lenient. As a foreigner, the young impostor could not be accused of treason, but he had nevertheless posed a severe threat to the king, and suppressing it had been troublesome and expensive. Yet, despite all this, Henry allowed the young impostor and his wife to stay at court, a situation that prevailed until Warbeck made a foolhardy bid for freedom. In June 1498, he was recaptured and put in the stocks to be publicly humiliated, before being imprisoned in the Tower of London.

In the Tower, Warbeck was held in a cell next to the Earl of Warwick, who had spent the whole of Henry's reign as a prisoner there. Within a few months, an anonymous informer reported that the two young men had hatched an audacious plot to burn down the Tower, escape to Flanders and place Warwick on the throne. Warbeck and Warwick were both put on trial and found guilty of treason. On 23 November, the self-proclaimed King Richard IV was carried on an open cart through to Tyburn gaol, the traditional place of execution for common criminals. There, he was allowed to read out his final 'confession' before being hung by the neck in front of a jeering crowd. 'Such,' said Francis Bacon, in his account of 1638, 'was the end of this little cockatrice of a king.'

Six days later, Edward, Earl of Warwick, was beheaded on Tower Hill. It has been suggested that Warbeck and Warwick never really plotted together, and that the rumours of their collaboration were in fact planted by Henry's agents. But, whatever the truth, Henry must have slept more soundly in his bed, secure in the knowledge that two major threats to his crown had been eliminated.

Edmund, Earl of Suffolk: The Last Pretender

If Henry had imagined that the death of the Earl of Warwick would put an end to all Yorkist claims to the throne, he was to be disappointed. Edmund de la Pole, Earl of Suffolk, now assumed the mantle of chief royal pretender. He was the brother of the Earl of Lincoln who had died at the Battle of Stoke Field, and he had nursed a particular grievance against the king since Henry had forbidden him from inheriting his dead father's dukedom. In 1501, Suffolk fled with his brother Richard to the court of the Emperor Maximilian I, and a group of nobles began to gather around them in Flanders.

After more than fifteen years on the throne, Henry once again faced the prospect of a Yorkist uprising, and this time he acted much more ruthlessly than before. Suffolk's relations who had remained in England were imprisoned and fifty-one men had their lands confiscated. In 1506, Henry negotiated with the Duke of Burgundy for the return of Suffolk to England, on condition that he would not be put to death. Henry was true to his word and spared Suffolk's life, but the earl spent the rest of his days in the Tower, and was executed in 1513 on the orders of Henry VIII.

Henry and the Nobles: Asserting Royal Power

Pretenders to the throne were far from the only problems that Henry faced. He was also surrounded by powerful magnates, who had become accustomed to wielding enormous influence over their monarch. If his new dynasty were to survive, Henry knew he had to change the balance of power. This meant reducing the power of the mighty barons. During his reign, he gradually cut down the size of the English nobility by severely limiting the number of new lords he created, and rarely raising nobles to a higher rank. New limits were put on the size of the nobles' private armies and Henry kept a careful watch on the marriages of his prominent subjects, exercising his right as their feudal lord to veto any alliance that threatened to create a dangerously influential powerbase.

From the very start of his reign, King Henry had used his royal right of attainder – or confiscation of lands – as a means of punishing disloyalty to the crown. (All those who fought against him at Bosworth Field had substantial portions of their estates attaindered.) In addition to this, any potentially rebellious nobleman had to pay a substantial bond to the crown as a promise of good behaviour. Henry also began to change the character of the Royal Council, a body that had always been dominated by the great lords of the land. During Henry's reign, only those nobles who proved to be efficient at their job (such as the Earl of Oxford) were retained, and a new class of administrator was introduced, picked from the ranks of the lesser nobility and professional classes. These new professional bureaucrats were often lawyers (men like Reginald Bray and Edmund Dudley) who took a pride in performing their royal duties with great efficiency. Men of noble birth discovered that they could no longer expect to wield power simply as part of their birthright. Instead, they had to earn the respect and trust of their monarch.

A Shrewd Head for Business

Henry VII's lasting image is that of a miser-king. Indeed,

it is believed that the line 'The king was in his counting house, counting out his money' in the traditional nursery rhyme *Sing a Song of Sixpence* refers to Henry Tudor and his obsessive piling up of wealth for the crown. It is certainly true that Henry played a hands-on role in the business of gathering taxes and his signature appears on many royal accounts.

Henry's overriding concern for the financial stability of the monarchy had its roots in an urgent need to fill the royal coffers after a long period of war. At the start of his reign, the royal finances were in a parlous position compared to those of his powerful subjects, with many crown assets neglected, overlooked or even pawned to the great lords of the land. Henry saw it as simple good housekeeping to claim back all the land owned by the crown and to reinstate the legal rights and taxes which his predecessors had allowed to lapse. He also made it his business to gain some personal control of his finances, developing the privy chamber – a smaller and more streamlined organization within the larger institution of the exchequer – and supervising the chamber's accounts with obsessive thoroughness.

Under the king's watchful eye, yield on crown lands was maximized. (These lands were extensive, comprising all the estates belonging to the Houses of York and Lancaster, as well as most of the Principality of Wales and the earldom of Richmond.) Outstanding debts were called in, money was raised from taxes to finance the king's military campaigns, and the local courts generated useful income through fines and confiscations. (Henry's legal system was mainly staffed with loyal men drawn from the local gentry.) Few of the king's subjects were exempt from his claims, as the royal agents, led first by Reginald Bray and later by Edmund Dudley and Sir Richard Empson, worked their way methodically through a tangle of ancient laws and rights, closing up loopholes and pursuing arrears. Ancient feudal dues were levied on nobles and the clergy, while the merchant classes had to pay substantial customs duties on imported goods such as wool, leather, cloth and wine. During his reign Henry also amassed a quantity of treasure for the crown in the form of gold and silver plate and jewels. The exile's obsession with portable wealth never left him, and he took great care always to appear on public occasions dressed in his finest robes and bedecked with jewels in an obvious display of wealth and majesty.

Powering Henry's money-making machine was a staff of loyal and efficient civil servants. Like any good businessman, Henry kept a close eye on his officials, presiding in person over meetings, ready to dismiss anyone who failed to meet his exacting standards. In his later years, Henry's concern for efficiency appears to have tipped over towards paranoia, as he even requested that some individuals taking up new jobs should pay a substantial bond that would be forfeited to the crown in the event that they failed to perform their role to the king's satisfaction.

By the end of his reign, Henry had not simply filled the royal coffers. He had also established a well-oiled royal machine for his descendants to inherit. Needless to say, such ruthless efficiency failed to win him the love of his people.

A Greedy King?

The Tudor chronicler, Polydore Vergil, wrote that by the closing years of Henry's rule 'the people were suffering not on account of their own sins, but on account of the greed of their monarch'. But did Henry really bleed his subjects dry? Historians today judge many of Henry's money-making measures to be efficient rather than extortionate. After the casual approach of his predecessors, Henry had a lot of ground to make up, and his new taxes must have seemed particularly harsh to subjects who had grown used to financial independence. However, there is plenty of evidence that the king's financial demands grew increasingly rapacious as his reign advanced. In particular, historians criticize Henry's extortion of enormous fines and bonds and his excessive customs taxes.

'Grievous burdens': the People Rebel

Henry's demands for money did not go unopposed. In 1489, Parliament granted him the right to raise £100,000 for his planned war against France (see page 71). The money was to be levied in a new way, as a general income tax, and this caused widespread resentment among Henry's subjects. Anger against the king was especially strong in Yorkshire, where farmers had just suffered a very poor harvest. In particular, the people of Yorkshire were especially incensed because the counties to the north of them were exempt from the tax as they were expected to defend the Scottish border. In April 1489 a band of the northern rebels rose up against the king under the leadership of the Earl of Egremont. For a short while it seemed that Henry had a serious rebellion on his hands, until the uprising was quelled by the king's loyal supporter, the Earl of Surrey. After this incident, there was no more trouble from the north, but the king failed to collect any more taxes for his war.

In 1497 Henry faced a second rebellion – this

time at the other end of his kingdom. Parliament had granted a tax to finance the English military response to a threatened invasion from Scotland (led by Perkin Warbeck), but the people of Cornwall refused to pay for a war so far from home. An army of rebels set off from Bodmin to march to London, prepared to fight for their rights. The rebels camped at Blackheath, in Kent, only a few miles south of the city of London, where they were met by the king's army. In the battle that followed, around 1,000 rebels were killed, and three of their leaders were later executed. The Cornish rebellion never posed a serious danger to the throne, but it was a matter of great concern that the rebels had managed to advance so close to London. Together with the Yorkshire uprising, it served as a clear warning to King Henry that he could not rely on his subjects to support his wars unquestioningly.

Looking Outwards: Trade and Exploration

Henry did not just apply himself to the amassing of

wealth for the royal coffers. He also made some astute moves to encourage English commerce. As Francis Bacon wrote, 'His thrifty mind could not endure to see trade sick.'The king worked hard to reverse the decline in English trade which had occurred during the Wars of the Roses. In those troubled years, cautious English merchants had developed the habit of relying on foreign ships to transport their goods, rather than investing in ships of their own, with the result that much valuable business had slipped out of their hands.

Henry saw the problem, and took decisive action to release the grip of foreign merchants on English trade. The Navigation Act of 1485–6 banned Englishmen from loading their goods onto a foreign ship if an English one was available. In 1489 another act was passed, forbidding foreign buyers from purchasing English wool before English merchants had bought all that they required. Henry also established good trading terms with Burgundy and Spain, although he was less successful in his dealings with the merchants of the Baltic. At the end of his reign, England was still a minor trading nation compared with Italy, Flanders and Spain but Henry had laid the foundations on which his successors could build.

Perhaps because he had spent so much of his youth by the sea, Henry had a passion for exploration which was remarkable for his time. Only Ferdinand and Isabella of Spain outshone the English king in their enthusiasm for the discovery of new lands, and it is not surprising that the Italian navigator, Christopher Columbus, approached the English king with his project to discover a new route to the east. Apparently, King Henry was intrigued by Columbus' ideas, but the plans were rejected by his Royal Council who judged that the Italian had severely underestimated the distances involved.

Columbus' discovery in 1492 was to change the balance of power in Europe, as Spain grew enormously rich from her trade with the New World. Watching the rise of Spain, Henry must have bitterly regretted the decision of his Royal Council, and this disappointment would have fuelled his enthusiasm to support the voyages of another explorer. John Cabot was an Italian captain who had arrived in England in 1495, and in the following year he approached King Henry with a plan. Cabot's aim was to sail west in search of new trading lands, taking a more northerly route than Columbus. Henry responded by providing a cautious advance of £50 and authorizing Cabot and his sons to 'sail to all parts, regions and coasts of the eastern, western and northern sea'. In the event, stormy weather rendered the expedition a disaster, but on his second voyage, in 1497, Cabot sighted land, and the banner of Henry VII was planted in Newfoundland. In 1498 Cabot set sail again from England but his fleet was lost in unexplained circumstances and he was never seen again. However, his explorations were continued by his son Sebastian.

In 1509, with King Henry's blessing, Sebastian Cabot sailed for the northern coast of America in search of the elusive north-west passage to Asia. Cabot's course carried him past the southern tip of Greenland, across the Davis Strait, and through a narrow opening into a vast area of water (which was in fact Hudson Bay). At this point drifting ice forced him to turn back, but Cabot was convinced that he had found a new route to the east, and he sailed back to England bearing the good news. By the time Cabot reached home, however, his royal master was dead. King Henry VIII did not inherit his father's interest in exploration, and it was left to Elizabeth I to pursue her grandfather's passion.

Foreign Friends, Foreign Enemies

'He was most fortunate in war, although he was constitutionally more inclined to peace than to war.' In these few words, Polydore Vergil ably summed up Henry VII's foreign policy. In an age when monarchs readily went to war, Henry made remarkably little use of his army as an instrument of foreign policy, relying instead on diplomacy to make England a significant player in European politics. By the time of his death, in 1509, England was widely respected abroad and Henry had secured a number of important treaties, ensuring his country's protection from invasion.

In the key opening years of his reign, Henry consolidated his position as king by securing agreements with England's traditional enemies – France and Scotland. His pacts with the French and Scottish rulers ensured a period of peace for England as it was established that neither power would support an invasion of England. This situation was complicated, however, when hostilities broke out between France and Brittany in 1487. Henry owed a personal loyalty to the Duke of Brittany, who had been his protector during his years of exile, but he was also eager not to antagonize France. At first, Henry compromised, sending conciliatory messages to King Charles VIII of France, while dispatching a small force of men to Brittany. But when France annexed Brittany, Henry realized that he was in a potentially dangerous position. Unwilling to wage a war against France which would almost certainly end in defeat, he decided instead on

Henry Tudor: A Contemporary View

The best contemporary description of King Henry VII is provided by the Italian historian, Polydore Vergil, in his history of Tudor England. Vergil only arrived in England in 1502, so his pen portrait describes the king in his late forties.

'His body was slender but well built and strong; his height above the average. His appearance was remarkably attractive and his face was cheerful, especially when speaking; his eyes were small and blue, his teeth few, poor and blackish; his hair was thin and white; his complexion sallow. His spirit was distinguished, wise and prudent; his mind was brave and resolute and never, even at moments of the greatest danger, deserted him. He had a most pertinacious memory. Withal he was not devoid of scholarship. In government he was shrewd and prudent, so that no one dared to get the better of him through deceit or guile. He was gracious and kind and was as attentive to his visitors as he was easy of access. His hospitality was splendidly generous; he was fond of having foreigners at his court and he freely conferred favours on them. But those

> *of his subjects who were indebted to him and who did not pay him due honour or who were generous only with promises, he treated with harsh severity. He well knew how to maintain his royal majesty and all which appertains to kingship at every time and in every place.'*

Polydore Vergil (1485–1537) *The Anglica Historia*

a clever game of bluff, and boldly asserted his right to the French crown. This ambitious claim was followed up by action in October 1492, when an English army crossed the channel and began to lay siege to the port of Boulogne.

On the surface, Henry's invasion of France seems a risky piece of bravado. In fact it was a perfectly calculated political move. Henry knew that King Charles was concentrating all his efforts on a major campaign in Italy and did not want the distraction of an invasion from the north. He had also planned the English attack for late in the fighting season to ensure that his troops did not have to fight for long. In the end the siege lasted just nine days before King Charles offered to negotiate with the English king. On 3 November the Treaty of Étaples was signed. Charles offered to pay the costs of the English invasion if Henry would withdraw his claim and his troops. The French king also promised not to support an invasion by Perkin Warbeck, while Henry agreed not to intervene on Brittany's behalf. The independence of Brittany had been sacrificed, but Henry had somehow emerged with honour from an otherwise unwinnable situation. He had proved, with no significant cost to his country, that England was a confident nation to be reckoned with.

Despite Henry's show of aggression – or perhaps because of it – relations between England and France remained cordial for the rest of his reign. Meanwhile, the king of Scotland, Henry's other long-term foe, agreed to a peace treaty in 1497. King James IV of Scotland had at first been seduced by the claims of Perkin Warbeck, but after the disastrous raid on England he wished to be rid of him. The Truce of Ayton expelled Warbeck from Scotland and assured non-aggression on both sides. It was a great achievement for Henry, as no such peace agreement between the two countries had been concluded since 1328. In 1503, the truce was sealed by the marriage of the young king of Scotland, James IV, to Henry's daughter Margaret.

Perhaps the greatest diplomatic triumph of Henry's reign was his alliance with Spain. As early as 1488, Henry had suggested a marriage between his eldest son, Prince Arthur, then aged 1, and the 2-year-old Catherine of Aragon, the youngest daughter of Ferdinand of Aragon and Isabella of Castile. This friendly advance paved the way, in 1489, for the two powers to sign the Treaty of Medina del Campo in which both sides promised not to invade one another or to form an alliance with France. Then, in 1492, two events took place that transformed Spain into a superpower. The kingdom was unified under the joint rule of Ferdinand and Isabella, and Christopher Columbus reached the

West Indies, claiming it for Spain. The newly formed Spanish kingdom rapidly amassed enormous riches through its trade with the New World while Henry continued to press for an alliance through marriage. For a time the Spanish rulers prevaricated while Henry's crown seemed at risk from pretenders, but in 1501 the marriage between Arthur and Catherine took place in St Paul's Cathedral in London. Their union marked a high point in Henry's reign, and the 44-year-old king must have looked forward to a more peaceful and prosperous future for his country, with England playing a part in the growing Spanish empire in the New World.

Henry Tudor the Man

What was Henry Tudor like, when he was not playing the role of king? Records of the time reveal that he was a keen reader, buying many printed books and manuscripts, building a library in his palace at Richmond, and acting as a generous patron to poets. Musicians of all kinds were welcomed into the royal household and Henry encouraged his children to play and enjoy music, spending 13s 4d on 'a lute for my lady Mary' (his daughter) and £2 'to the princess's string minstrels at Westminster'. Unsurprisingly, for such an expert in the art of diplomacy, he was a keen player of cards, dice and chess, and he also enjoyed tennis and hunting. Away from his counting house, the king appears to have been a contented family man, devoted to his wife and children, and with a hearty appetite for life, enjoying May games, play acting and Morris dancing. For a man with a reputation as a miser, he was also capable of surprising gestures of extravagance, once spending £13 on a leopard for his royal menagerie and £30 'for a little maiden that danceth'.

In matters of religion, Henry seems to have been conventionally pious. He had a particular devotion to the Virgin Mary and was the proud possessor of a number of relics, including a leg of St George. In his will, the king requested the saying of a thousand Masses for his soul and funded the construction of the magnificent

Sweating Sickness

The virulent disease known as the sweating sickness swept through England during the Tudor period, killing tens of thousands, especially in the cities of London, Oxford and Cambridge. The first epidemic occurred in 1485, just as Henry VII was claiming the throne, and the last outbreak was in 1551, after which the disease appears to have vanished completely. The disease began very suddenly with cold shivers, giddiness, headache and severe pains in the neck and shoulders. This stage was followed by hot sweats, rapid pulse and intense thirst. The final stage was exhaustion and collapse, and an irresistible urge to sleep. Unlike the plague, sweating sickness had no outward symptoms, and was unusually rapid in its course through a victim's body. Death frequently occurred within hours of the onset of the first symptoms, and people told stories of friends who had been 'merry at dinner and dead at supper'.

Historians have failed to identify the exact nature of the sweating sickness, but it was probably a form of typhoid. It was certainly spread by the grossly unhygienic living conditions in Tudor towns and cities. In 16th-century England water supplies were often polluted, sewerage was almost non-existent and towns were crowded, stinking slums — especially in summer. City streets were filled with household rubbish of every kind, the contents of chamber pots and the droppings of horses, dogs and chickens. Rats, fleas and mice teemed everywhere and lice infested beds, clothes and people's hair.

Unsurprisingly, no effective treatment was found for the sweating sickness. Doctors tried bleeding their patients, or confined them in sealed rooms, bundled up in blankets. Other cures combined herbal remedies with sorcery and charms. King Henry VIII, who was mortally afraid of the sweating sickness, even devised his own 'king's cure' made from a mixture of herbs and wine, which he pressed on all his friends and relations.

Lady Chapel at Westminster Abbey to house his tomb.

At the time of Prince Arthur's wedding, in 1501, Henry and Elizabeth had four living children. Prince

Edmund had died in the previous year, at the age of 2, but the royal couple still had two fine sons, 16-year-old Arthur and 10-year-old Henry, and two daughters, Margaret, aged 12, and 2-year-old Mary. On Prince Arthur's wedding day, King Henry must have looked on proudly as the young Prince Henry escorted the Spanish princess down the aisle of St Paul's Cathedral, delivering the young bride to his clever and serious older brother.The wedding celebrations lasted for more than a week but eventually the newly-weds set off for their new home in Ludlow Castle on the Welsh borders. There Arthur took up his duties as Prince of Wales, but within five months, tragedy had struck. Catherine and Arthur both contracted the deadly sweating sickness, and while the sturdy Catherine survived, her more delicate husband died.

Henry and Elizabeth were devastated by the death of their beloved first-born, although they both made brave attempts to comfort one another.Apart from their overwhelming personal grief, there was also a very real anxiety about the future of their dynasty. In an age when death could strike suddenly, the royal couple now only had a single male heir. Queen Elizabeth gently reminded her husband that they were both still young enough to have more children (she was 35 and Henry 44), and within a few months Elizabeth was pregnant again.

On 2 February 1503, Elizabeth gave birth to a daughter, Catherine, but within a few days of the birth, the queen became seriously ill. Elizabeth died on her birthday, 11 February, and the baby princess lasted only a few days more. Henry was stricken by grief. Having given detailed orders for the funeral, he 'privily withdrew to a solitary place, and would no man should resort to him'.

The End of a Reign

The year 1503 must have been a bleak time for Henry Tudor. In the summer, he escorted his daughter Margaret to Scotland to be married to King James IV, returning home to just two children – Henry and Mary.

Without the diverting company of his wife and first-born son, the royal finances became Henry's major obsession, as he urged his officials on to ever more rigorous money-making schemes. He was also much concerned with questions of marriage. Following the death of his queen, the 46-year-old king automatically became one of Europe's most eligible bachelors. There was considerable political advantage to be gained through the right union, not to mention the chance to father more heirs to the throne. Henry was always the consummate political player, and so, with somewhat indecent haste, he began to look around for a suitable match.

Henry's first marriage candidate was his son's widow, Catherine of Aragon, who had remained in England after her husband's death. However, this suggestion was swiftly vetoed by Catherine's parents, whose response – it seems – was largely motivated by the fear that Henry Tudor might die, leaving their daughter stranded in a foreign land with very little power. Instead, the

Spanish rulers favoured a marriage contract between Catherine and Prince Henry and this was duly agreed by King Henry on behalf of his son. Next, the king turned his attention to Joanna, Queen of Naples, sending an ambassador to check on her appearance, but eventually he rejected her as insufficiently wealthy to be his bride. A third alternative arose in the person of Queen Joanna, widow of Philip, Duke of Burgundy, who became Philip I of Castile. However, she proved to be mentally unstable.

In fact, Henry's search for a bride was destined to fail. To complicate matters further, young Henry's betrothal to Catherine of Aragon ran into trouble when Queen Isabella of Castile died in 1504, resulting in the drastic reduction of her daughter's inheritance. Following Queen Isabella's death, relations between Spain and England deteriorated rapidly as Henry began to see the Spanish princess as a liability. In one of the most shameful episodes of his reign, Henry stopped Catherine's allowance and entered into a long and acrimonious wrangle with King Ferdinand about the size of his daughter's dowry. Caught between the two squabbling monarchs, Catherine was left penniless, forced to pawn the plate that was part of her dowry in order to buy sufficient food for herself and her ladies in waiting.

Royal Requirements

When King Henry VII considered marriage to the Queen of Naples, he encountered a serious problem: he had no idea what his prospective bride was really like. Unwilling to rely on the flattering reports of Queen Joanna's countrymen, he decided to send his own ambassador to check her out. Henry's list of points to be investigated makes fascinating reading. In addition to reporting on the lady's height and general appearance, the unfortunate ambassador was commanded to inform his king on the length of her neck and the size of her breasts, arms and feet. Henry was also anxious to be told whether the queen had bad breath or any hint of a moustache!

By the time he entered his fifties, Henry's health had started to fail. In the spring of 1509 he fell ill and on 21 April he died, aged 52, at his palace at Richmond, not far from London. A magnificent funeral was held in Westminster Abbey, but few people mourned the passing of the old king. Despite being one of England's most able monarchs, both at home and abroad, Henry had never won the hearts of his subjects. By the end of his reign, his people had grown resentful of his financial demands, and all hopes were focused on his handsome son. Sir Thomas More expressed the feelings of most of his countrymen when he wrote, 'This day is the end of our slavery, the fount of our liberty; the end of sadness, the beginning of joy.' Thanks to the unceasing efforts of his father, the young King Henry VIII inherited a prosperous, peaceful and well-run kingdom. England was well-respected abroad and he had more money in his coffers than any other ruler in Europe. The Tudor dynasty had truly come of age.

Chapter 3
THE PROMISE OF GREATNESS – YOUNG HENRY VIII

Everybody recognizes the popular image of King Henry VIII. Seeming more like an ogre than a man, he stands with legs apart and arms akimbo, staring out defiantly at the world. He is the tyrant who married six times, who dared to defy the pope, and who sent hundreds of subjects to their deaths, including former ministers and even two of his wives.

But there is another Henry. The young man who was crowned king in 1509, four days before his 18th birthday, was widely recognized as the most promising prince ever to ascend to the English throne. Tall, slim, handsome and athletic, he was an able scholar and a skilled musician who also loved to dance, joust and hunt. He was devout in his religious observances and devoted to his new wife. So how did such a promising young prince turn into the monster of his later years?

In order to understand the character of King Henry VIII, we should first look for clues in his childhood.

'Nature could not have done more for him.'

If contemporary accounts are to be believed, the young King Henry was dazzlingly handsome. A Venetian visitor wrote that 'His majesty is the handsomest potentate I ever set eyes on', noting Henry's unusual height and splendid build and commenting on his glowing auburn hair and his pink, round face so delicate 'that it would become a pretty woman'. Another commentator was even more enthusiastic, claiming that 'Nature could not have done more for him. He is much handsomer than the king of France, very fair and his whole frame admirably proportioned.'

Second-Best Son?

Prince Henry was born on 28 June 1491 in the royal palace at Greenwich. As the third child of King Henry VII, he was welcomed into the world with far less pomp and ceremony than his older siblings had enjoyed. Five years earlier, the arrival of Prince Arthur had been stage-managed by the king as a stunning piece of Tudor propaganda, with both the birth and christening taking place in the ancient city of Winchester in a deliberate bid to link the Tudor dynasty to the seat of the fabled King Arthur. Princess Margaret's birth, in 1489, had also been a very public event, largely because it occurred just a day before Arthur's investiture as Prince of Wales. The princess was christened in St Margaret's Church in Westminster and carried back in triumph to Westminster Palace. By contrast, Prince Henry's birth was a low-key affair, taking place in one of the king's many out-of-town homes. His christening was held in the Friars' Church, close to Greenwich Palace, and while it was an occasion for much royal pageantry, it passed almost unrecorded by the chroniclers.

As the king's second son, Henry received a very different upbringing from his older brother. From his earliest days, Prince Arthur was assigned a nursery establishment of his own. Henry, on the other hand, shared his nursery with his older sister Margaret. Within the royal nursery, the infant Henry was allotted his own set of rooms: a sleeping chamber, a reception room and two smaller rooms for his servants. Following the usual practices of the time, a wet nurse was responsible for breastfeeding him for his first two years, and he was also cared for by two 'rockers', whose duties including rocking Henry's cradle and dealing with his laundry.

In July 1492, a third royal infant – Princess Elizabeth – joined Margaret and Henry. As the only boy in the royal nursery, Henry was probably singled out for special treatment. Certainly, by the time he was 3 years old, he was a lively and confident child, more than ready to face his first public appearance.

Dreams of Knighthood

Prince Henry was catapulted onto the public stage by a disturbing threat to his father's throne. Three years earlier, the impostor Perkin Warbeck had made the outrageous claim that he was the Duke of York, the younger of the princes imprisoned in the Tower.

When he was supported by some of the most powerful figures in Europe, King Henry VII decided to take action. In order to counteract Warbeck's claim, the king resolved to create a genuine Duke of York in the person of his second son. He would stage a ceremony that would proclaim the power of the Tudors to the whole of Europe – and the star of the show would be Prince Henry.

The great occasion took place in November 1494, when Henry was just 3 years and 4 months old. It began with a parade of mounted lords riding from Fleet Street to Westminster through streets lined with cheering crowds. And heading the parade – to everyone's astonishment – was the young prince, riding unaided on the back of a warhorse. At Westminster, a grand banquet was held, in which Prince Henry played the part of a squire waiting on the king, and this was followed by the traditional knighting ceremony. In the company of twenty-two other candidates for knighthood, Henry was first given a ritual bath, and then dressed in a hermit's robe before being led in a solemn procession to a chapel. There, he had to keep vigil until the early hours before he was allowed a few hours' sleep in preparation for the knighting ceremony in the morning. All of this was overwhelming enough, but the climax came on the following day when he was appointed Duke of York in the Palace of Westminster in front of all the great nobles of the land.

After these stirring ceremonies, the young Prince Henry must have returned to his nursery with a new sense of confidence. As historian David Starkey points out, he must have been thrilled by the thought that he was now a knight, just like the heroes of his adventure stories. But despite his triumphs Henry was still little more than a toddler, and he needed to concentrate on the serious business of getting an education.

Early Education

Henry's schooling started early. When he was just 4½, his father paid for 'a book bought for my lord of York'.

Evidently he could read and write at an early age, and by the time he was 6, he was judged old enough to begin serious learning. Henry's personal tutor was Master John Skelton, an accomplished poet, who was also expert in Latin grammar and learned in classical literature. Henry's later skill in writing Latin and his ability to turn his hand to verse must have been partly due to his first teacher. Skelton was also known for the exuberance of his poems, which were sometimes scurrilous in nature, and something of his rumbustious style seems to have rubbed off on his royal pupil.

By the time of Henry's 9th birthday, there had been several changes in the royal nursery. In 1495, his sister Elizabeth died, at the age of 3. Henry was then 4 years old – grown up enough to miss his baby sister and to register his parents' grief (Henry and Elizabeth spent a small fortune on a funeral and monument for their much loved daughter). In the following year, the queen gave birth to another daughter, named Mary, and when Henry was 7 years old, Prince Edmund was born.

Edmund died before his second birthday, leaving Henry surrounded by his sisters.

A vivid description survives of Prince Henry and his siblings. In 1499, the Dutch scholar Desiderius Erasmus accompanied the author and statesman Sir Thomas More to the royal palace at Eltham. 'For there,' Erasmus wrote, 'all the royal children were being educated, Arthur alone excepted, the eldest son. When we came to the hall, all the retinue was assembled.... In the midst stood Henry, aged nine, already with a certain royal demeanour; I mean a dignity of mind combined with a remarkable courtesy. On his right was Margaret, about eleven years old, who afterwards married James, King of the Scots. On the left Mary was playing, a child of four. Edmund was an infant in arms.' Confronted by this royal group, Sir Thomas More stepped forward and presented Henry with a piece of writing, but Erasmus had arrived empty handed. This omission was noted by Prince Henry, and later in the evening, when the two scholars were dining with the royal family, the prince sent Erasmus a note requesting 'the gift of some writing from his pen'. Erasmus rose to the challenge and within a few days had delivered a short collection of poems. It is not known how Henry responded to the scholar's offering, but Erasmus was clearly impressed by the self-possession of the young prince. Here was a boy who was eager to read new texts but who also expected fitting tributes from the great scholars of his age.

A Wedding and a Funeral

While Henry and his sisters were growing up together, their older brother Arthur was leading a very different kind of life. As the heir apparent, he had always been kept apart from the rest of the royal brood, and at the age of 6, he was sent to Ludlow Castle on the borders of Wales. In Ludlow, the infant Prince of Wales embarked on his serious training for kingship, presiding over his own Royal Council, just as his father did in London. It must have been a lonely life for a young boy, but unlike his ebullient younger brother, Arthur was quiet and scholarly and he took his royal responsibilities very seriously.

At the age of 3, Prince Arthur had been promised in marriage to the Spanish princess Catherine of Aragon, and when he reached 13, the couple were married by proxy with the Spanish ambassador standing in for the young girl. Following this ceremony, Arthur and Catherine corresponded in Latin for two years until it was decided that Arthur was old enough to wed in person. When the couple finally met, they discovered to their distress that they were unable to understand one another, as they had each learned different pronunciations of Latin. However, Arthur reported to his parents that he was immensely happy to 'behold the face of his lovely bride'.

Ten days later, on 14 November 1501, the royal couple were married in St Paul's Cathedral. Their marriage marked the high point of Arthur's princely career, but it was his 10-year-old brother who stole the show. Prince Henry had the honour of leading the bride down the long cathedral aisle, with all eyes upon them. Later, at the wedding feast, Henry defied convention by removing his doublet and dancing energetically in his shirt.

After the celebrations, Arthur returned to Ludlow with his new wife, but within five months he was dead. Henry was not yet 11 when he stepped into his older brother's shoes as the heir apparent to the throne.

Henry, Prince of Wales

At first, Prince Henry's life does not appear to have changed dramatically. Following his brother's death, Henry was granted the title of Prince of Wales but there was no formal coronation and he was not sent to Ludlow. Instead, he continued to live quietly with his sisters, moving on to the next stage of his education. By the time Prince Henry was 11, John Skelton had been replaced by Master John Holt, a professional schoolmaster, and when Holt died, another schoolmaster, William Hone, took his place. Under their tutelage, Henry underwent an intensive course of study, acquiring a thorough knowledge of classical texts, history and theology. The Prince was coached in modern languages, particularly French, and studied music, becoming a skilled performer and singer. Physical instruction was not forgotten, as Henry was assigned his own master at arms to train him in jousting and the arts of war. Henry developed into a fine all-round sportsman, enjoying hunting and riding, and excelling in wrestling, archery and tennis. Whenever he could, he indulged his passion for dancing, and, before he was 12, he had already developed a dangerous enthusiasm for gambling with dice.

Learning To Be King

For the first few years following Arthur's death, Henry must have felt as though he were in limbo. Probably his father was too distracted by his grief at the loss of his beloved first-born to have much time for Henry. But then another tragedy struck the family when Queen

Henry the Musician

Henry VIII's reputation as a gifted musician is well-founded. While he was probably not the author of the famous tune 'Greensleeves', he did compose at least two five-part masses, a motet, a large number of instrumental pieces, songs and rounds, including the song 'Pastime with Good Company'. An accomplished singer and musician, Henry could sight-read musical notation with ease and was a skilful player on the lute, the virginals and the recorder. Throughout his reign, he was a generous patron to musicians, inviting many performers to his court, who would sometimes play to the king for four hours at a stretch.

Elizabeth died in childbirth in February 1503. This second loss devastated the king, and also had the result of focusing his attention on his heir. In January 1504, a solemn ceremony was held to recognize Henry as Prince of Wales. A few weeks earlier, 14-year-old Henry had left his sisters to live with his father in order to study kingship at first hand. For the next five years, until the king's death, Prince Henry lived in his father's shadow. Deprived of the company of other young people, he was installed in a room next to the king's that could only be reached through his father's chamber. When a Spanish ambassador visited the English court, he reported in horror that Prince Henry was completely dominated by his father and grandmother, speaking to them alone on public occasions.

It must have been a desperately difficult time for Henry. Condemned to spend most of his time with his ailing and unhappy father, the teenage prince must have sorely missed the company of his sisters and his male sporting companions. The royal court in the later years of King Henry VII's reign was not a cheerful place, and as his father's famous meanness became more and more evident, Prince Henry must have absorbed an atmosphere of general resentment.

The young prince was also tangled up in some highly acrimonious marriage machinations. The obvious bride for him was Catherine of Aragon, who had been left stranded in England after Arthur's death. King Henry was clearly unwilling to relinquish such a prize and, in 1503, a marriage treaty was signed. However, there were difficulties to be overcome, as the pope's permission had to be sought for a union with a dead brother's widow. In July 1504, the pope indicated his willingness to grant a dispensation, and the couple were formally betrothed in a small private ceremony. The formalities were barely over, however, before the news arrived that Catherine's mother was dead. With the death of Queen Isabella of Castile, Catherine's inheritance was drastically reduced, making Prince Henry's marriage much less financially attractive to his father. Just before his 14th birthday, Henry followed his father's orders and repudiated his betrothal. Meanwhile Catherine was kept in the dark, and remained convinced that she was still promised to Prince Henry.

Two years after her betrothal to Prince Henry, the king cut off Catherine's allowance and suggested that she should come and live at court as an economy measure. The result was total humiliation for Catherine and enormous embarrassment for Prince Henry. His potential wife was living uncomfortably close to him but was rarely allowed to see him. As Catherine complained bitterly about her father-in-law, 'He regards me as bound and his son as free.'

Henry the King

Henry's long period as monarch-in-waiting came to an end in April 1509 with the death of his father. As custom demanded, Henry remained in the Tower of London until after his father's funeral, but one of his first actions as soon as Henry was buried was to marry Catherine of Aragon. The reasons underlying Henry's marriage are difficult to unravel. Did he feel a sense of obligation towards the young woman to whom he had long been promised in marriage? Was he emulating his older brother by marrying Arthur's widow? Or perhaps he was genuinely in love? Whatever his motives, Henry and Catherine were married in a quiet ceremony at Greenwich. It was the first step in the preparations for a spectacular coronation for Henry and his queen, to be held in Westminster Abbey on 24 June.

'Virtue, Glory, Immortality'

The general delight at the coronation of the new king is summed up in a famous letter from Lord Mountjoy to his tutor Erasmus.

'Heaven and earth rejoices; everything is full of milk and honey and nectar. Avarice has fled the country. Our king is not after gold, or gems, or precious metals, but virtue, glory, immortality.'

On the morning of their coronation, Henry and Catherine processed to the abbey under a canopy of richly embroidered tapestries, dressed in their finest robes on which diamonds, rubies and other precious stones flashed and sparkled. After a solemn service lasting several hours, the new king and queen retired to a banquet that lasted until nightfall. The following days were filled with jousting tournaments, dancing, pageantry and concerts. Henry had begun his reign in style.

Right from the start, it was clear that the young king would not follow slavishly in his father's footsteps. Just two days after his coronation, Henry ordered the arrest of two of his father's hated ministers, Sir Richard Empson and Edmund Dudley. The pair were tried for treason and put to death, after a confession had been forced from them. In the opening months of his reign, Henry also reversed many of the bonds that his father had imposed on the nobility – a hugely popular move that won him the support of the English aristocracy.

The first Christmas and New Year of Henry's reign were marked by another tournament – and this time Henry took part himself, riding incognito in a closed helmet, before revealing himself to the delighted crowd. Queen Catherine looked on proudly from the royal pavilion, already pregnant with the king's first child. Everybody hoped that there would soon be an heir to complete Henry's happiness. Catherine gave birth at the end of January, but the child – a girl – was two months premature and stillborn. However, a second pregnancy proved more successful and on New Year's Day 1511, a son and heir was born – to the great delight of King Henry and his loyal subjects. In London, bells were rung, bonfires were lit and cannons fired repeated salutes. The christening of the infant Prince Henry took place on the following Sunday, with representatives from all the great royal houses of Europe in attendance. King Henry went on a pilgrimage to the shrine of Our Lady at Walsingham in devout gratitude for the gift of a son and heir, returning in time for a joust to be held in honour of his wife. At the tournament King Henry played a leading role, winning several prizes. It must have seemed to his people that fortune was smiling on their new king, but ten days after the jousting ended, the infant Prince Henry sickened and died. It was a bitter blow for the 20-year-old king. It also marked the beginning of Henry's longing for a son that would become an obsession as the years wore on.

Going To War

Henry had put on a terrific public spectacle in the opening months of his reign, but the burning question remained – what exactly was he going to do as king? The obvious choice for Henry was to go to war. As an active young man skilled in martial arts, he looked back with envy to the great campaigns of the Black Prince and Henry V. Henry longed to prove himself in battle like the famous kings of the past – and he was especially keen to square up to England's old enemy, France.

Accordingly, Henry set about picking a quarrel with France. Soon after becoming king, he made a public pronouncement that he would soon launch an assault against the French King Louis XII, and a few weeks later he deliberately insulted an envoy from the French court. Within a matter of months, Henry had undone all the good will created by his father's careful negotiations. But there still remained an insuperable obstacle to war – Henry could find no ally to join in his attack. The young king also faced determined opposition from the Royal Council. Most of the council members had served under his father and they supported the old king's policy of careful diplomacy and peacemaking. King Henry VIII would clearly have to bide his time.

In fact, an opportunity for war arrived in 1511, when Pope Julius II proclaimed a Holy League against France, enlisting the help of Spain and the Holy Roman Empire to drive the French out of Italy. Henry joined the League and began to plot with Spain for a joint Anglo-Spanish conquest of Aquitaine (a duchy in south-western France that had once been held by the English crown). The enterprise turned out to be a miserable failure, largely due to lack of Spanish support, but a second campaign against France was planned for the following year. This time, King Ferdinand of Spain agreed to a two-pronged attack, with the Spanish forces attacking Aquitaine while Henry led an assault on Normandy.

By the autumn of 1512, preparations for war were well under way in England. Henry paid regular visits to the docks to watch his warships being built, taking special delight in the warship *Henry Grace à Dieu* nicknamed *Great Harry*. Shipbuilding was to remain one of his lasting passions and Henry is often credited with the founding of the Royal Navy, expanding the Tudor fighting force from a mere five to 53 ships. In the early spring, a military camp was established in Calais, which had remained under English control since the Hundred Years War, and in June King Henry himself set sail for France. Travelling with the king was a vast royal entourage, including bishops and nobles, ministers of the crown, minstrels, players, heralds, trumpeters, clerks and over 300 other members of the royal household. There was also a vast amount of royal clothing, golden goblets and plate and an enormous carved wooden bed. For three weeks Henry presided in his royal tent, planning the details of his campaign, until eventually the army set off to do battle. On 16 August, Henry's army won the Battle of the Spurs at Guinegate, capturing the small town of Thérouanne, and on 24 September, they gained the important prize of Tournai after an eight-day siege. Henry returned from France in triumph, but in fact a far more impressive victory had been won at home. While Henry had been busy in France, King James IV of Scotland had seized the opportunity to launch an attack on the northern borders of England. On 9 September, the Scottish and English armies met in bloody battle at Flodden Field. The fighting lasted for three hours before the English gained the upper hand, slaughtering many of the Scottish noblemen present, and finally King James himself. With the death of King James, the Scottish threat receded for several decades. James had left an infant son in the care of his mother, Henry's older sister, Margaret, but he was merely 1 year old. King Henry would not have any more trouble from Scotland until the closing years of his reign.

The Meeting of the Kings

King Henry had imagined that his French campaign would resume in the following spring, but within a year the complex game of European diplomacy had moved on. The pope was no longer at war with France and Henry's chief adviser, Thomas Wolsey, persuaded him that the way to gain the most advantage for England was to form a new alliance with France. One of the best ways to cement such an alliance was through marriage and so, in October 1514, Henry's younger sister Mary was married to the widowed King Louis XII of France. From Mary's point of view it was not an appealing union. Louis was three times her age, pock-marked, gouty and toothless, while she was widely acknowledged to be one of the most beautiful princesses in Europe, but she did not have to suffer his presence for long. Eleven weeks after their marriage, Louis died (reputedly worn out by his efforts in the marriage bed) and he was succeeded by his cousin's son, Francis I. In the young French king, Henry recognized a potential rival. Like Henry he was tall, athletic and ambitious, and he was just 20 years old. Henry and Francis might either be very dangerous enemies or very powerful friends – and Henry decided to extend the hand of friendship.

Negotiations proceeded slowly until, in 1519, a momentous meeting of the two leaders was agreed. As a signal of his serious intent, Henry promised not to shave until they met and Francis quickly reciprocated. Even when Henry failed in his promise, confessing that his wife insisted he shave off his beard, good relations did not suffer. Instead it was gallantly declared that the love between the two kings was 'not in the beards but in the hearts'.

The meeting which became known as the Field of the Cloth of Gold was one of the most glittering occasions in European history. It was deliberately staged on neutral ground, between the English territory of Calais and the kingdom of France, and both nations vied to outdo one another in magnificence as they constructed vast pavilions of cloth encrusted with golden thread and jewels. Even the ground was spread with embroidered carpets, making it a literal field of golden cloth. Commentators at the time described the temporary city as the eighth wonder of the world – and this was just a stage for the elaborate ritual of the royal encounter. On Corpus Christi Day, 7 June 1520, a cannon sounded the signal for both kings to advance from their respective encampments. Mounted on their chargers and dressed in full knightly regalia, Henry and Francis galloped towards each other, halted, and embraced three times, before dismounting, embracing once again and retiring to a pavilion. This was the signal for the festivities to begin. For the next fortnight, the field provided a glorious arena for a succession of banquets, concerts, jousts and other entertainments. The two kings jousted and tilted together, and one day, when the wind was high, they even wrestled and danced. There was an awkward moment in the wrestling match when Francis threw Henry to the ground, but Henry recovered his dignity by winning at archery. Finally, on 24 June, the sport came to an end. A parting banquet was held and the two kings vowed to build a chapel of peace on the spot where they had met.

Was the meeting at the Field of the Cloth of Gold

simply a gigantic folly, or did it have some lasting effect? It certainly added lustre to the reputations of Henry and Francis. It may also have helped to avoid conflict for a few years, although by the 1520s both monarchs were making warlike threats. But one thing is certain. The eighteen-day extravaganza was ruinously expensive – and Henry was rapidly running out of money.

Henry and the Cardinal

The organizing genius behind the Field of the Cloth of Gold was Thomas Wolsey. The son of a butcher from Ipswich, he had been an outstanding secretary to one of Henry VII's advisers, and he was picked by the new young king to be his almoner (in charge of a large proportion of the royal funds). Wolsey rapidly gained Henry's confidence and rose to become Lord Chancellor in 1515. At the same time, he was ascending the ranks of the Church. In 1514 he became Archbishop of York and in the following year Pope Leo X appointed him as a cardinal.

The Perfect Wife?

When the scholar Erasmus visited the Tudor court in 1520, he wrote in glowing terms of the royal couple, praising Henry and Catherine's 'strict and harmonious wedlock' and adding 'Where could one find a wife more keen to equal her admirable spouse?' And Catherine certainly had many admirable qualities. She was unusually intelligent, having been thoroughly schooled in the classics (Erasmus rated her scholarship more highly than the king's), but she always deferred to the judgement of her husband. Unfailingly gracious and smiling, she played the part of a dutiful wife with enthusiasm, praising Henry's prowess in dancing, jousting and wrestling. In her spare time, Catherine busied herself making and embroidering shirts for her husband, and when the king was away at war, she worried about his health and safety and fretted over whether he had enough clean linen. When Henry departed for the war in 1513, Queen Catherine assumed the role of regent, coping calmly with a Scottish invasion. She even made a rousing speech to the English captains urging them to remember that 'English courage excelled that of all other nations'.

In Wolsey, Henry discovered a man of great intelligence, clear judgement and an enormous capacity for work. The king must have also recognized a confidence and ambition that matched his own, but while Henry loathed the paperwork that came with the role of king, Wolsey appeared to revel in it, sending out dozens of documents every day. Within a very short time, Henry had made Wolsey his right-hand man, ceding enormous responsibility to him, and rewarding him generously for his efforts. While Henry rode and hunted, jousted and made merry, Wolsey divided his time between the exchequer and the chancery and also made time for delicate foreign negotiations. During the twenty years that he worked for Henry, Wolsey generated a constant stream of documents and letters to be read and signed by the king, who was notoriously disinclined to put pen to paper.

Cardinal Wolsey's most pressing concern was money. While King Henry VII had piled up wealth, his son squandered it. Henry Tudor had left £1,250,000 in the royal coffers (the equivalent of around £375 billions today), but Henry VIII set about draining them rapidly. Each year, hundreds of pounds were spent on clothing the monarch, feeding his court and paying his servants, and thousands on his palaces, which grew in number during Henry's reign from a dozen to fifty-five. War was especially costly and Henry's campaigns in France in 1513 are estimated to have cost around £600,000. One of Wolsey's greatest achievements was to revolutionize the English taxation system so that tax was based on a valuation of the taxpayer's wealth. This more efficient form of taxation helped to raise money for the King's foreign expeditions, but it was still not enough. As Henry's reign progressed, the need for funds would become the driving force behind his policies.

Concern for the royal finances didn't stop Wolsey from spending money himself – and his abiding passion was building. He created a spectacular country home for himself at Hampton Court, south-west of London, and founded Cardinal College (now known as Christ

Church) in Oxford. Following Wolsey's fall from favour in 1529, when he opposed Henry's attempt to divorce his queen, his properties passed to the king and Hampton Court became a favourite royal residence.

In his special relationship with the king, Thomas Wolsey established a dangerous precedent. Throughout his reign Henry would rely on a few trusted advisers to help him make all his decisions. It must have been both flattering and immensely exciting to be so close to the king, but such power came at a terrible cost – as Wolsey was to discover when he dared to intervene in Henry's love life.

Sir Loyal Heart?

Henry's marriage to Catherine of Aragon lasted for twenty-four years (from 1509 to 1533), and for the first few years he showed every sign of being in love. As a newly-wed, Henry wore Catherine's initials on his sleeve in jousts, called himself 'Sir Loyal Heart' and paid his wife elaborate compliments. Even after he had been married for five years, the king was still keen to race home from his victories in France in order to present his wife with the keys to the cities he had captured.

By 1514, however, there was evidence that the king's attention had started to stray. During the New Year's festivities, a lively young woman named Bessie Blount caught his eye, and in 1519 she bore Henry a son. (The boy – named Henry Fitzroy – was brought up at court as a royal prince in the accepted manner of the time.) Around the year 1521 Henry became romantically involved with Mary Boleyn, a lady in waiting at court, but their affair seems to have come to an end by 1525.

None of this was a cause for undue concern. Romantic adventures outside the royal marriage bed were commonplace in Henry's time, and even his virtuous father was said to have fathered an illegitimate son. In the case of Henry VIII, however, there was an added problem. As the years wore on, it seemed that Catherine might fail in her most important wifely duty – to provide her husband with a son.

Dangerous Lady Anne

In 1525, Henry had been married to Catherine for sixteen years. He was still in his prime, at 34, while Catherine, now aged 40, had become a portly, middle-aged matron. It is not surprising that she had lost her figure – or that Henry looked elsewhere for sexual satisfaction – as she had been pregnant for much of their married life. It has been estimated that Catherine conceived as many as ten times, but only one living child – Princess Mary – survived. All her other pregnancies ended in tragedy, as she either miscarried, gave birth to a stillborn child or produced an infant that died within a few weeks. The birth of a healthy daughter in 1516 had raised Henry's hopes of a future male heir, but he slowly realized that his hopes were unfounded. In 1518, at the age of 33, Catherine had her last recorded pregnancy, which resulted in another stillborn child. By the time she was 40, it was clear that the queen had reached the end of her childbearing years.

Into this tricky situation came Anne Boleyn – the

sister of Henry's former mistress, Mary. Anne was born into a leading aristocratic family with close connections to the English crown. Her father had worked as a diplomat for King Henry VII and she had been educated in the Netherlands, before serving as maid of honour first to Margaret of Austria and then to Queen Claude of France. While at the French court, Anne studied theology and became a keen follower of fashion. The young woman who arrived in the English court, aged around 20 (her exact birth date is not known), was unusually well-educated, cultured and politically aware. She was a skilled dancer – one commentator wrote appreciatively 'Here was a fresh young damsel that could trip and go' – and was quick and witty in conversation. While most people agreed that Anne was no great beauty, she was immensely striking, with her thick dark hair, long elegant neck and eyes so dark that they were almost black. She also had enormous personal charm, which she had learned to use in order to achieve exactly what she wanted.

Rivals in Love

The grandson of Sir Thomas Wyatt related a story of the rivalry between Sir Thomas and King Henry for the attention of Anne Boleyn. According to his story, Wyatt was flirting with Lady Anne when he playfully snatched a locket from her purse. Around the same time, Henry had taken one of Anne's rings to wear on his little finger. A few days later, Henry was playing bowls with a group of lords and a dispute arose between the king and Wyatt about a winning throw. Pointing with the finger which bore the lady's ring, Henry smiled and said 'I tell thee it is mine.' Not to be outdone, Wyatt took out the locket. 'First give me leave to measure it,' he said, before using the locket to measure the distance between the ball and the jack. The story ended with Henry striding away, muttering angrily that he had been deceived.

Henry's infatuation with Anne Boleyn really blossomed in the spring of 1526. At that time, Anne was also toying with the affections of the poet and courtier, Sir Thomas Wyatt, and the rivalry between the two men must have helped to ignite Henry's passion as the king soon became determined to win her favours. Confronted by an importunate royal suitor, Anne retreated, resisting all his attempts to make her his mistress. It is hard to tell whether Anne held out against Henry's demands out of a genuine fear of the consequences, or as a means to entice him further. But, whatever her motives, King Henry was well and truly hooked. And when Anne recognized the extent of her power, she played her most risky card of all. Did Henry love her enough to make her his queen?

Anne's timing was perfect. By the time the couple met, Henry had already started to ask himself whether his lack of heirs was in fact a punishment from God. A passage in the Old Testament forbade a man to marry his brother's widow lest he and his wife be cursed. Now Henry returned to this passage obsessively. Back in 1504, Pope Julius II had granted him a special dispensation to marry Catherine, but was it really valid?

And could Henry use a biblical passage as the excuse to end his union with his wife? Henry resolved that he would do his utmost to persuade the pope to grant him an annulment. Then he would be free to marry Anne.

In 1527 Henry embarked on a determined campaign to persuade the pope of the justice of his cause. This set him on a course that would eventually lead to a total break with Rome – but that still lay several years in the future.

The End of an Era

By 1527, the glory days of Henry's early reign were over. His financial problems were worsening. He was on the brink of ending his marriage to a queen who was widely admired. And he had fallen in love with a volatile, highly ambitious young woman. At 36, he was active and vigorous, but he was no longer the slim, athletic hero who had ascended the throne – and he still lacked a son and heir. Henry must have wondered what the future held in store for him.

Chapter 4

TURMOIL AND TYRANNY – THE LATER REIGN OF HENRY VIII

The second half of King Henry's reign was a truly tumultuous period. In the space of just fifteen years, the king married five times, broke free of the pope's control, stripped the English monasteries of their wealth, put numerous of his subjects to death, and faced domestic uprising and foreign invasion. However, in 1527, he was still married to Catherine of Aragon, and his first priority was to set himself free so that he could make Anne Boleyn his queen.

Quarrels with the Pope

Henry was desperate for the pope to annul his marriage, but it seemed that everything was ranged against him. In 1527 Pope Clement VII had become the prisoner of Catherine of Aragon's nephew, Emperor Charles V, and so he was naturally reluctant to take Henry's side. While Clement prevaricated, Henry became dangerously impatient, blaming Cardinal Wolsey for the delay, and even accusing him of plotting to force Anne Boleyn into exile. In 1529, with Anne's encouragement, Henry stripped Wolsey of his seals of office. The following year, Wolsey was arrested on charges of high treason, but he died in custody before he could be brought to trial.

Wolsey's place at court was taken by Sir Thomas More, an eminent lawyer and scholar and trusted friend of the king. Henry believed he could rely on More's support, and at first his new chancellor championed his cause, backing legal opinion that Henry's marriage to Catherine had been unlawful. However, as Henry persisted in his defiance of the pope, More became increasingly uneasy.

Changes were also afoot at court. By 1531, Henry had openly rejected Catherine of Aragon, banishing her from her royal apartments and even depriving her of the company of her daughter, Mary. Catherine's place was rapidly taken by Anne Boleyn, who busied herself with schemes to gain more power. When the old Archbishop of Canterbury died, Anne persuaded Henry to replace him with Thomas Cranmer, the Boleyn family chaplain.

Sir Thomas More 1478–1535

Sir Thomas More was a lawyer, theologian, philosopher and statesman and one of the outstanding figures of the Tudor age. As well as playing a key role in the king's government, he was the author of *A History of King Richard III* and several works of theology. His most famous work, *Utopia*, is still read today. It presents a fictional account of a perfect society in which all land is owned communally, private property does not exist, men and women are educated alike and there is almost complete religious toleration.

More was a man of many facets. As a leading humanist, he was deeply involved in the revival of classical learning, but he was also a devout Roman Catholic who launched vituperative attacks on Martin Luther and punished religious heretics with death. More's unwavering loyalty to the pope propelled him into a fatal quarrel with his king. In 1534, he was summoned to swear his agreement to Henry's Oath of Supremacy, and when he refused, he was imprisoned in the Tower. Three months later he was executed for treason.

She also gave her support to a clever young lawyer called Thomas Cromwell, who devoted his efforts to promoting the interests of the king.

In 1532 Cromwell brought an act before Parliament claiming royal supremacy over the English Church. It was a bold move, designed to invest the king with the powers he needed to defy the pope, and it was the last straw for Thomas More. Horrified by such an open insult to papal authority, More resigned as chancellor, leaving Cromwell as the king's first minister. King Henry was set on course for a major confrontation with Rome.

In mid-January 1533, Anne Boleyn discovered she was pregnant. This added urgency to the situation and events began to move rapidly. On 25 January, Henry and Anne were married secretly. On 28 May, Archbishop Cranmer ruled that the marriage of Henry and Catherine was null and void. On 1 June, Anne was crowned Queen Consort. Eight years after she had first attracted the king's attention, Anne Boleyn had finally achieved her aim. She was queen of England and she was expecting the king's child. Meanwhile, Henry awaited the reaction of the pope.

Pope Clement's response was unequivocal. He roundly condemned Henry's marriage to Anne, and ordered the disobedient king to take back his former wife on pain of excommunication. The threat was designed to bring Henry swiftly back in line, but the English king stood firm. He was determined to make Anne his legal queen, even if it meant breaking away from Rome. In November 1534, the English Parliament passed the Act of Supremacy, with its ringing declaration that the King was 'the only Supreme Head in Earth of the Church of England'. From then on, the English Church would never be answerable to the pope again.

Anne the Queen

The long-awaited marriage did not prosper. Once Anne was crowned queen, the charms that had originally commended her to Henry soon began to pall. What had once seemed charming liveliness, now appeared to

Henry and the Monasteries

Between the years 1536 and 1541, King Henry gave orders for the systematic looting and destruction of English convents and monasteries. This dramatic purge, known as the Dissolution of the Monasteries, was partly motivated by a desire for reform. (It was common knowledge that many monks and nuns enjoyed a luxurious lifestyle, funded by their great estates.) However, the driving force behind the dissolution was financial. By the mid-1530s the royal coffers were empty, and the English abbeys were legendarily wealthy, owning more than a fifth of the country's landed wealth, as well as fabulous treasure in the form of statues, silver and gold.

Acting through Thomas Cromwell and his agents, Henry emptied the abbey buildings, seized their treasure and confiscated their lands. Most of the abbey lands were redistributed among the landed gentry who had to pay heavy taxes to the crown.

him to be wilful disobedience, while the queen's high spirits too often degenerated into vicious outbursts of temper. Henry hated to be crossed in any way and Anne's constant attempts to involve herself in the business of government began to enrage him, as well as making her many enemies at court. As the new queen of England, Anne also failed to win the hearts of the English people, who remained stubbornly devoted to Catherine. But the greatest test of all was whether Anne could provide her husband with an heir...

As the time of his wife's confinement approached, King Henry began to plan extravagant celebrations. Everyone was confident that the queen would have a boy – the astrologers had predicted it and so had the physicians – and preparations were put in place for a magnificent tournament to welcome the baby prince. The queen was installed in a splendid bed and the birth went smoothly – but, contrary to predictions, Anne gave birth to a girl. On 7 September 1533, Princess Elizabeth was born. Henry cancelled the tournament and sank into a black depression.

It was the beginning of the end for Anne. While the

royal couple still enjoyed brief periods of calm, there were frequent sharp exchanges, and contemporaries reported on much 'coldness and grumbling' between husband and wife. In 1534, Anne became pregnant again but her child was stillborn. Meanwhile, Henry had his eye on another young lady at the court – the pleasingly quiet and demure Jane Seymour.

In autumn 1535, Anne conceived for a third time. No longer secure in her husband's affections, she must have felt that everything depended on her ability to deliver a son – but fortune was against her. In late January, Henry fell from his horse and was knocked unconscious for several hours, causing great concern for his life. This worrying event was followed within a week by a second disaster, when Anne miscarried, probably as a result of her concern for the king. The queen was hysterical with grief – especially as the baby she had lost was a boy – while her husband was coldly furious. As Anne retired to her chamber to recover her strength, King Henry began to speak of witchcraft. His wife was

Henry VIII – Catholic or Protestant?

King Henry VIII has often been claimed as a major figure in the Protestant movement, coupled with such revolutionaries as Martin Luther and John Calvin. Yet despite his dramatic break with Rome, Henry never saw himself as a Protestant. As a young king, he was a devout Catholic, praying to relics and going on pilgrimages, and in 1521 he was even moved to write a *Defence of the Seven Sacraments*, defending the pope's authority and attacking Luther's claims as heretical. This spirited piece of Catholic propaganda earned Henry the gratitude of Pope Leo X, who granted him the title of Defender of the Faith (a title the English monarch still retains today). Throughout his life, Henry never renounced the teachings of the Roman Catholic Church, even while condemning to death those devout Catholics – such as Sir Thomas More and Archbishop Fisher – who dared to defy his own religious authority.

Yet, in spite of Henry's avowed Catholicism, the Church of England soon acquired a character of its own, as Henry ordered his priests to preach against superstitious relics and to remove most candles from their altars. Following royal orders, many shrines and pilgrimage sites were suppressed, and a new prayer book, written in English for the laity, omitted most of the prayers addressed to saints. In 1539, Henry took a significant step to make the Christian religion more accessible to the people of England, when copies of an English translation of the Bible were distributed to parish churches, with instructions that they should be placed in 'some convenient place' for all to see and read.

really a sorceress, he claimed, and she had deliberately used her evil charms to lure him into marriage.

The End of Anne

King Henry had supplanted an unwanted wife before, and now he planned to do so again. With somewhat indecent haste, he moved Jane Seymour into new quarters to be close to him, while Jane's brother, Thomas, was awarded the prestigious Order of the Garter. (This was partly a deliberate snub to Anne, whose brother, George Boleyn, had been refused the honour.) After many years as the king's favoured mistress, Anne suddenly found herself in the position of the wronged wife. But unlike Catherine of Aragon she refused to bear her fate patiently.

All Anne's ragings were to no avail, however. Once Cromwell was sure that she should be disposed of, he moved swiftly to set the legal machinery in motion. On May Day 1536, five men, including George Boleyn, were arrested for treason and charged with having sexual relations with the queen. The following day, Queen Anne herself was placed under arrest and imprisoned in the Tower of London. The prisoners were tried for adultery, incest and high treason, and despite a notable lack of evidence all were found guilty and condemned to death. Early in the morning of 19 May 1536, Anne was led to meet her death by execution. In a final speech before she knelt at the block, she accepted her fate without complaint, She also asked God to 'save the king and send him long to reign over you, for a gentler

Was Anne Boleyn a Witch?

King Henry's accusation that Anne had bewitched him sparked off a storm of rumours that she was a witch. The enemies of the queen were quick to compile a list of her physical deformities, claiming that she was unnaturally tall, that she had a sixth finger, and had strange warts and growths on her body that could have been a witch's teats. They also claimed that Anne had given birth to a deformed male foetus in 1536. The question of witchcraft was raised in Anne's trial but was not included in the final list of charges against her.

At the time of Anne's trial, there were growing fears of witchcraft, and King Henry's Act Against Conjuration, Witchcraft and Dealing with Evil was subsequently passed in 1542. This was followed by a second, more draconian, law in the reign of Elizabeth designed to punish by death anyone who should 'use, practise, or exercise any Witchcraft, Enchantment, Charm, or Sorcery, whereby any person shall happen to be killed or destroyed'. Such broad charges were notoriously difficult to prove and hundreds of innocent victims were accused of witchcraft and then put to death.

nor a more merciful prince was there never: and to me he was ever a good, a gentle and sovereign lord.' It was a gracious end to a stormy life.

Gentle Jane

One day after Queen Anne's execution, Henry became engaged to Jane Seymour. Ten days later they were married quietly in the chapel of one of the king's London homes. With remarkable speed, King Henry had embarked on his third marriage.

As a royal lady in waiting, Jane Seymour came from a very similar social background to Anne Boleyn. Like Anne, she was descended from a noble family (they even had a great-grandmother in common), but, unlike Anne, Jane had not been highly educated. Much to Henry's relief, his new wife did not take an active interest in politics, preferring household management and needlework, at which she excelled. In appearance too, Henry's second and third wives were direct opposites: while Anne was dark-haired and fiery, Jane was pale, blonde and gentle. Under Queen Jane, the royal court became a calmer, if duller, place, governed by a strict sense of decorum. Gone were the extravagant fashions introduced by Anne and in their place were strict regulations for court dress – even down to the number of pearls to be sewn onto a lady's skirt. Jane also introduced a new spirit of gentleness into the royal household. As a devout Roman Catholic, Jane sympathized with Henry's daughter Mary, who had been brought up by her mother in the old faith. She made Mary welcome at court and encouraged Henry to show more kindness to his elder daughter.

Queen Jane also performed the essential duty of becoming pregnant. By June 1537, it was known that she was with child, and on 12 October she gave birth to a long-awaited son and heir. Henry was not with the queen at the time of her delivery, but he hurried back joyfully to Hampton Court. In a mood of great exultation, Henry embarked on a round of celebrations and on 15 October a grand christening ceremony was held for the infant Prince Edward. Soon afterwards, however, the mood in the court darkened as it was reported that the queen was ill. She had developed 'child-bed-fever', or septicaemia, a type of blood-poisoning that was the cause of most maternal deaths in the Tudor period. With no effective treatment for infection, there was no real hope for the queen and she died twelve days after the birth of her son.

Jane was buried in St George's Chapel, Windsor Castle – the only one of Henry's six wives to be given a queen's funeral. When Henry died ten years later, he was buried beside her in the royal tomb.

Uprisings Against the King

During the time that Henry was married to Jane, he faced one of the most frightening episodes of his reign. In 1536 he had embarked on his campaign to dissolve the monasteries, targeting those establishments that were evidently corrupt. Henry must have assumed that his loyal subjects would not object to his methods, but he was wrong. People of all classes felt that their religious traditions were endangered, while the landed gentry were alarmed by Henry's policy of confiscation, fearing that their own lands were also under threat. Underlying these responses was a general resentment of the king's taxes, a suspicion of his ministers – especially Thomas Cromwell – and a sense of disillusionment with his policies, particularly his treatment of Catherine of Aragon. All these factors contributed to a northern uprising known as the Pilgrimage of Grace.

In October 1536, around 9,000 men mustered at York under their charismatic leader, Robert Aske, a local landowner and lawyer. The movement was well funded by donations from wealthy landowners and churchmen, and extremely well led. Under Aske's command, a collection of men from a diverse range of backgrounds was transformed into a disciplined army. Aske also had the inspired idea of naming the rebellion the Pilgrimage of Grace, and assuring that all who joined it would gain spiritual reward for their part in returning the king to the path of virtue.

On 21 October, the Pilgrims seized Pontefract Castle. By this time their numbers had swollen to around 35,000, posing a significant threat to the king. Faced with this serious military challenge, Henry ordered the Duke of Norfolk and the Earl of Shrewsbury to ride to Pontefract and confront the rebels. However, they could only raise about 8,000 men. Henry would have faced almost certain defeat in battle had not Robert Aské favoured negotiation rather than force. With supreme skill, the Duke of Norfolk managed to persuade Aske and the other leaders that he was sympathetic to their cause, and escorted them to London to open negotiations with the king.

In early December 1537, a group of leading Pilgrims presented 24 articles to the king. The articles amounted to a demand for Henry to reverse his religious policies and to punish Cromwell and other unpopular councillors. To the Pilgrims' delight, King Henry agreed that their demands would all be considered in the near future, and also granted a pardon to all who had joined the pilgrimage. Aske took the good news back to his followers: King Henry had been led astray, but now he would return to the path of righteousness.

But Henry proved false to his word. Once he was sure that the Pilgrims were safely disbanded, the king began to wreak his revenge. One by one, the movement's leaders were summoned to trial. The promise of pardon was withdrawn and they were found guilty of treason and condemned to death. Even when Jane Seymour pleaded with her husband to pardon the men, Henry was adamant. All the leading rebels were put to death, and Robert Aske's body was hung in chains from the walls of York Castle as a vivid warning to anyone who might dare to defy the king. From that time on, there were no more uprisings in England. King Henry had shown his strength, and he now felt free to pursue his policies with even more determination. But he had forfeited the love and trust of his people.

Hans Holbein: King's Painter (*c*.1498–1543)

Hans Holbein was the son of a German painter, and is often known as Hans Holbein the Younger to distinguish him from his father. He began his career in Basel, producing designs for murals, stained glass and printed books. In 1526 he travelled to England in search of work, and by the 1530s he was working for Anne Boleyn and Thomas Cromwell. In 1535, Holbein became King's Painter to Henry VIII. In this role, he produced portraits and festive decorations and also designs for jewellery, serving dishes and other precious objects.

Holbein's art belongs to the Northern Renaissance school in its realism and attention to detail, but is highly individual in style, and filled with mysterious symbols and allusions. His portraits of the royal family and nobles provide a vivid record of the Tudor court in the reign of King Henry VIII. Henry held Holbein in very high esteem and is reputed to have said, 'Of seven peasants I can make seven lords, but not one Holbein.'

'The Flanders Mare'

Henry must have been saddened and shocked by the death of his queen, but this did not stop him seeking an immediate replacement. Within a few days of the queen's funeral, Thomas Cromwell was already on the lookout for a new bride for the king. As one of Europe's leading monarchs, Henry was in a position to make a union of great advantage to his country. In an age of high infant mortality, it was also expedient that he fathered as many sons as possible.

This time, Cromwell looked to the royal houses of Europe for a potential queen, and he had soon set in motion the complex processes of foreign diplomacy. Over the next two years at least nine candidates were considered for the role of Henry's fourth wife, and five sat for portraits by the painter Hans Holbein. Eventually, however, it was decided that an alliance with a German duchy would bring the greatest advantages. The Duke of Cleves ruled over a wealthy and strategically important state, and had succeeded in maintaining independence while forging strong relations with his neighbours, the Lutheran Princes. Since Henry's break with Rome, England had been dangerously isolated, and a link with Protestant Germany would provide some much-needed security.

Accordingly, ambassadors were dispatched to report on Anne of Cleves and Holbein was sent to paint her portrait. The reports from Flanders were not entirely encouraging: the 23-year-old Anne was not well-educated, although she did like sewing and playing cards. She could not sing or dance and could converse only in German. Comments on Anne's appearance were non-committal, with envoys praising her honesty and modesty 'which appeareth plainly in the gravity of her face'. Under the circumstances, Henry must have examined Holbein's portrait carefully, but this did not offer any serious cause for alarm. The woman in the picture appeared rather plain and solemn, but generally pleasing in appearance. Evidently, Henry was sufficiently reassured to sign the marriage contract, and in late December Anne set off for England.

On New Year's Day in 1540, Anne's ship arrived at the port of Rochester, and Henry rushed down to Kent to spy on his bride-to-be. In the company of some gentlemen companions – all disguised in multi-coloured cloaks – he climbed the stairs to her chamber to deliver a New Year's gift. Henry had been anticipating this moment for months, but he was in for an unwelcome surprise. She was not the beautiful young girl that he had imagined – and he felt deeply betrayed. Back in Greenwich, Henry rounded on Cromwell for trapping him into an unwanted union. 'She is nothing so fair as she hath been reported,' he complained, 'I like her not.' The marriage was postponed for two days while the king tried to wriggle out of his contract, but there was no escape. England could not afford to offend Germany and the wedding duly went ahead on 6 January 1540.

The king's fourth marriage was never consummated. Henry claimed frankly that his initial repugnance for

'Is this not enough?'

While Henry was complaining that he could not consummate his marriage to Anne of Cleves, it seems that the lady herself remained blissfully unaware of the problem. Her ladies in waiting reported that Anne had told them 'When he [Henry] comes to bed, he kisses me and taketh me by the hand, and biddeth me "Goodnight, sweetheart," and in the morning, kisses me, and biddeth me, "Farewell, darling." Is this not enough?'

his bride had grown even stronger on their wedding night, complaining of the 'hanging of her breasts and looseness of her flesh', and though the king and queen lay together regularly in the following months, he roundly asserted that his wife was still 'a maid'. Within a few months of his marriage, Henry was planning a divorce – on the combined grounds of non-consummation and the existence of a previous marriage contract for Anne. This time there was no need to turn to any higher authority to bring the marriage to a conclusion, and

Thomas Cromwell c.1485–1540

Thomas Cromwell was a blacksmith's son who rose to the highest office in the land. As a young man, he travelled around Europe, working as a merchant and a soldier and becoming fluent in Latin, Italian and French. Around 1512, Cromwell returned to England and studied law, securing the prestigious post of legal secretary to Cardinal Wolsey.

As Wolsey's star fell, Cromwell gained the confidence of the king, and in 1532 he was appointed as Henry's chief minister, a position he held until 1540. Despite his lack of clerical office, he played a key role in the English Reformation, encouraging Henry's break with Rome and masterminding the Dissolution of the Monasteries. A brilliant administrator, he worked to modernize English government, reducing the privileges of the nobility and the Church, and was also the architect of a series of acts uniting England and Wales.

Cromwell's downfall came when he pushed the king into a humiliating marriage with Anne of Cleves for the sake of an alliance with Protestant Germany. Henry's fury at Cromwell led to his arrest on charges of treason and he was executed at Tyburn on 28 July 1540.

in early July Parliament declared the union null and void.

To Henry's great relief, Anne proved to be more han happy to go along with his plans. When requested, she penned a letter confirming that her marriage had not been consummated, addressing the king as 'brother' and signing herself as 'sister'. She also showed no willingness to return home, despite her brother's urgent requests. In the seven months that Anne had been in England, she had grown to like the place, developing friendly relations with both Henry's daughters (Mary was then 24 years old, just one year older than Anne, while Elizabeth was a winning 7-year-old). She was granted a generous allowance by the king and several fine homes from which to choose (including the Boleyn's ancestral home of Hever Castle in Kent), but she preferred to spend her time at court, enjoying her position as 'the King's beloved sister', growing plump and cheerful and developing a taste for English beer.

Changes at Court

There was another reason behind Henry's eagerness to part with Anne. Within a few weeks of his marriage, the king had spotted a new young lady at the royal court. Catherine Howard was appointed as a maid of honour to Anne of Cleves towards the end of 1539. She was around 19 years old (her exact birth date is not known), short, plump and vivacious and already experienced in the art of seduction. She was also the pawn of a group of highly ambitious courtiers, led by her powerful uncle Thomas Howard, Duke of Norfolk, and his political ally, Stephen Gardiner, Bishop of Winchester. As upholders of the old faith, they hoped to gain more influence over the king, thus counteracting the pro-Protestant policies of Thomas Cromwell, and even possibly securing the chancellor's fall from grace.

By the spring of 1540, royal gifts and favours had begun to flow towards Catherine and her relatives. It was also noticed that Henry and Catherine were making frequent visits to the Howard and Gardiner family homes. Howard and Gardiner swiftly made use of their new access to the king to bring about Cromwell's downfall, and on 10 June Cromwell was arrested and taken to the Tower of London. It is not known how Henry was persuaded to consent to Cromwell's arrest, but he was certainly angry about Cromwell's part in his marriage to Anne of Cleves and he probably came to believe that Cromwell had plans to turn England into a fully-blown Protestant country.

On 9 July, King Henry's marriage to Anne was declared null and void. This opened the way for Norfolk and Gardiner to make their next move. They led the Royal Council in begging the king 'to frame his most noble heart to love' in order to secure 'some more store of fruit and succession'. By then, King Henry was thoroughly infatuated with Catherine and there were also suggestions that Catherine might be pregnant, making a legal union extremely urgent. On 28 July, only 19 days after the annulment of his fourth marriage, Henry and Catherine were married at Oatlands Palace in Surrey. On the same day, Cromwell was executed in the Tower. King Henry had entered a new and uncertain period in his life.

A Rose Without a Thorn?

King Henry was besotted with Catherine Howard. He described her as his 'blushing rose without a thorn', smothered her with kisses, and showered her with gifts. In the first ecstatic months of his marriage, Henry presented Catherine with a constant stream of jewellery, dresses, castles, titles and manors. In return, Catherine played the role of a loving and obedient wife.

As a highly impressionable young woman, Catherine was overwhelmed by the majesty of the king. But the reality of Henry the man was less appealing. At the time of his marriage Henry was 49 – easily old enough to be Catherine's father. He was also short-tempered, overweight and ill. His girth had increased alarmingly since he had entered his 40s. It has been estimated that he weighed about 135 kg (around 21 stone) and a suit of armour made for the king in 1540 reveals that he had a 137-cm (54-inch) waist and a 145-cm (57-inch) chest. Back in the 1520s, Henry had developed varicose ulcers, and these had gradually become chronic. At times, the ulcers became dangerously inflamed causing bouts of fever and extreme pain, which did nothing to improve the king's temper.

At first, the king made strenuous efforts to keep up with his young bride, rising daily between five and six, hunting until ten, and dancing and feasting at night, but by the spring of 1541, he had succumbed to fever. One of the ulcers, deliberately kept open by doctors in order to maintain the king's health, suddenly closed and Henry's physicians feared for his life. In his illness, Henry grew savage, lashing out at all around him. He began to suspect his advisers of treachery and to express regret for the death of his 'faithful servant' Cromwell. The king's venom was also turned on his subjects, and he vowed that he would 'shortly make [them] so poor that they would not have the boldness nor the power to oppose him'.

Catherine Howard was not well equipped to cope with her husband's black moods – or even to conduct herself wisely at court. As a young girl, she had been consigned by her parents into the care of her step-grandmother, the widow of the second Duke of Norfolk. In the dowager duchess's glittering household Catherine's education was neglected, but she was acquainted with romance from an early age. When she was about 15 years old, she enjoyed a serious flirtation with her music teacher, Henry Mannox. In her later confessions, Catherine maintained that this relationship was unconsummated, but 'being but a young girl I suffered him at sundry times to handle and touch the secret parts of my body'. Two years later, she had a second, more serious, affair with Francis Dereham, a secretary in the duchess's household, and the pair became lovers, addressing one another as 'husband' and 'wife'. After the dowager duchess learned of the affair, Dereham left for Ireland but the couple may have intended to marry on his return. All these early experiences gave

Catherine a dangerous taste for intrigue and romance – and must have fuelled her distaste for her husband's efforts in the marriage bed. Certainly, within a year of their wedding, she had begun to look for satisfaction elsewhere. By the spring of 1541, she was flirting with Thomas Culpepper, one of the gentlemen of the privy chamber (a personal attendant to the monarch). She had also been persuaded to find a place in the king's household for her old lover, Francis Dereham.

Catherine was playing a very risky game. By the summer of 1541 she and Thomas Culpepper had embarked on a passionate affair, conducted right under her royal husband's nose. When the king and queen embarked on a royal progress to York, Culpepper managed to steal into the queen's bedchamber at almost every stopping place, aided by Lady Rochford, one of the queen's older ladies in waiting. Throughout August and September, Henry remained blissfully unaware of his wife's adultery. However, the members of his Royal Council were not so easily deceived. They had been informed of Catherine's previous relationship with Dereham, and had also received reports of the queen's affair from one of her ladies of the bedchamber. The council resolved to warn the king and, in early November, Archbishop Cranmer handed Henry a document while he was at Mass. At first the king denounced the document as a pack of lies, but evidence was soon supplied, including a love letter to Culpepper in the queen's distinctive handwriting. Faced with such incontrovertible proof, Henry broke down and wept.

Dereham and Culpepper were sent to the Tower of London where they made a full confession before being put to death. Meanwhile, Catherine was charged with treason, and stripped of her title as queen. For the next three months, she was held as a prisoner at Syon Abbey in Middlesex before being transported to the Tower. On 13 February 1542, Catherine faced execution on Tower Green, along with her lady in waiting, Lady Rochford. Less than two years after marrying Henry, she had become the second of his wives to lose her head.

Henry's Wars

It would be sixteen months before King Henry married again. In the meantime, he faced some serious challenges from his old enemies – the French and the Scots.

Ever since his first French campaign, Henry had harboured ambitions of winning more land in France, and in 1542 he began to prepare for another campaign. This time the Holy Roman Emperor Charles V was Henry's ally, but the alliance proved shaky right from the start. Despite a prior agreement that the English army would march on Paris, Henry headed instead for the Channel port of Boulogne, a prize he had long desired. Under the leadership of the Duke of Suffolk, the English succeeded in seizing Boulogne on 18 September 1544, but it would prove to be an isolated victory. On the day that the port surrendered, Charles V signed a peace treaty with France. The war with France was over and the English troops went home. Henry had spent a fortune preparing his army for war, but had very little to show for it.

The capture of Boulogne had one serious consequence – it spurred the French to take revenge. News of a planned invasion reached Henry in the winter of 1544, and he gave orders for a series of fortifications to be constructed on England's south coast. In the event, the French campaign of spring 1545 was an abject failure, due to a combination of incompetence and bad weather. Held back by adverse winds, the French ships ran out of supplies before they even had a chance to engage conclusively in battle and they were forced to withdraw ignominiously to France. The most notable casualty on the English side was the much-prized warship, the *Mary Rose*, which keeled over and sank in Portsmouth harbour while sailing out to engage the French vessels. Apart from the loss of the *Mary Rose*, the English had escaped astonishingly lightly, although the financial costs had been enormous. Henry had spent two million pounds on his French campaign – the equivalent of ten years' normal government expenditure.

King Henry's dealings with Scotland were equally unimpressive. By 1541, Henry was fearful that France and Scotland might unite to invade England, and he summoned the Scottish king to meet him in York. King James V of Scotland was the son of his sister Margaret, and Henry expected instant obedience from his nephew. When James repeatedly failed to appear, Henry realized that he would need a show of force to bring Scotland into a state of submission. Accordingly, the Duke of Norfolk was dispatched to lead a series of raids across the Scottish borders. Unfortunately for Henry, however, preparations had been minimal, and Norfolk's troops were forced to return much earlier than planned. Instead of demonstrating strength, England had seemed weak. This encouraged James to launch his own raid on the south as an assertion of Scottish power.

The result was the Battle of Solway Moss, fought on 24 November 1542. This time Henry's fortunes improved as the Scots were even more poorly led than the English. Somehow, a well-equipped Scottish army, numbering over 15,000 men, managed to become trapped in a bog, suffering a humiliating defeat at the hands of an English force of around 3,000 troops. The Scottish army was decimated and the English managed to capture many leading nobles. Just a fortnight later a dispirited King James V died, leaving a baby daughter (who was to become Mary, Queen of Scots) and a desperately vulnerable kingdom.

This was Henry's great opportunity. Had he acted decisively, it is probable that his army could have seized control of Scotland. Then he could have claimed the infant Princess Mary as his ward, and asserted his right as feudal overlord of the King of Scotland. But instead Henry favoured diplomacy – possibly because his army was already overcommitted in France. Heaping gifts on the Scottish nobles captured at Solway Moss, Henry sent them home charged with the task of advancing the English cause. Unsurprisingly, very little happened, while many months were wasted in an attempt to negotiate a marriage contract between Prince Edward and the infant Princess Mary. While negotiations dragged on, the Scots took the opportunity to rebuild their army, before deciding at the end of the year not to ratify the treaty after all. Realizing that he once again needed a show of force, Henry launched a punitive raid on Edinburgh, setting fire to the city. But this turned out to be a disastrous move. Instead of cowing the Scots, the vicious English attack united them in fierce opposition to their southern neighbours and strengthened their determination to form an alliance with France. By the time of Henry's death, Scotland was more hostile to England than ever before. Henry had squandered his winning position and left a difficult legacy for his heirs to deal with.

The King's Last Wife

By 1543 – the year of his last marriage – King Henry was 52 years old and far from well. He had grown extremely fat and was in constant pain from the ulcers on his legs. Walking was very painful, and although he still went riding, he had to be winched into his saddle. At home in the royal palaces, the king was carried from room to room and hauled upstairs by machinery. The role of king was lonely and demanding, particularly since the death of Thomas Cromwell. Henry was in desperate need of a companion to support and comfort him in his declining years – and he found the ideal woman in Catherine Parr.

Catherine came from a respectable landed family. Both her parents had served at court, but her father had died when Catherine was about 4 years old, leaving her mother, Maud, to bring up their three children. Nevertheless, Catherine received a sound education and was raised to be courteous, level-headed and gentle. At 17, she was married to a young nobleman who died within three years, leaving Catherine a widow at the age of 20. Her second marriage was to a widower, Lord Latimer of Snape Castle in Yorkshire, and for the next nine years she cared for her husband, showing great kindness to his children. When Latimer died in 1543, Catherine was 31. Childless and with a decent fortune, she at last felt able to follow her heart, and developed a strong affection for Sir Thomas Seymour, the brother of Henry's third wife, Jane Seymour. But just as Catherine had glimpsed the chance of happiness with Thomas, King Henry began to take an interest in her. Torn between love and duty, Catherine chose duty and married the king.

Catherine was married to Henry in the chapel at Hampton Court, just as Jane Seymour and Anne of Cleves had been before her. Unlike some of Henry's former weddings, this was not a private ceremony and both Henry's daughters were invited. Catherine took her role as stepmother very seriously, extending the hand of friendship to Mary, and concerning herself with the education of Elizabeth and Edward, then aged 9 and 5. Catherine engaged some of the leading scholars of the age to supervise the royal children's education. She also embarked on her own study of Latin, struggling to keep up with her royal stepchildren. (The 8-year-old Edward later sent Catherine a solemn letter congratulating her on her efforts.) During the years that Catherine was queen, the royal residences became cheerful places, as she enjoyed dancing and music, employed a company of jesters and kept pet greyhounds and parrots. Nor did the new queen neglect her religion, spending many hours at her devotions and even compiling a book of prayers and meditations. As one courtier put it, 'Her rare goodness made every day like a Sunday, a thing hitherto unheard of in royal palaces.'

By 1544, Queen Catherine had become more of a nurse than a bedfellow to the king, moving out of her queenly apartments and establishing herself in a small room beside her husband's bed chamber, ready to comfort him whenever he needed her. It must have been a thankless task, as Henry often raged in pain, and the stench from the infected ulcer on his thigh was said to be appalling. But Catherine had already nursed one husband carefully, and she performed her duty selflessly. In his last marriage, Henry had at last chosen wisely and well.

The End of a Reign

The last few years of Henry's reign were not notably successful. As the ailing king struggled to rule without the support of a close adviser, his financial problems multiplied. He also became increasingly tyrannical, consigning many royal servants to their deaths. In the poisonous atmosphere of fear and suspicion that washed around the court, rumours of plots abounded and punishment was swift. Even the mighty Duke of Norfolk was not exempt from the king's wrath, and was due to be beheaded on the day when King Henry died.

By December 1546, the king's health was failing, although he made heroic efforts to rally his strength. Even when he finally took to his bed, it was clear that he was not yet ready for a peaceful end. Right up until his dying hours, Henry fretted and plotted about the future of his realm. Prince Edward was only 9 years old, and it would be at least six years before he could rule for himself. Fearing that his son would become the pawn of powerful political factions, Henry had drawn up a will that specified that England should be ruled by a Regency Council, all of whom possessed equal authority. Now, as his strength ebbed away, Henry kept making alterations to the members of the Regency Council in a desperate attempt to exert control over the situation, even from beyond the grave. Eventually, however, his iron will failed and he died on 28 January 1547 in the Palace of Whitehall. Eight days later, the royal funeral was held at St George's Chapel, Windsor, and Henry was buried in the Lady Chapel beside Jane Seymour, as he had requested. Work had begun on an elaborate royal tomb (which had originally been intended for Cardinal Wolsey) but it was never completed, and Henry shares a burial slab with the ill-fated King Charles I.

Henry's Legacy

When King Henry died, at the age of 55, the royal coffers were empty and his subjects were chafing under his rule. The English nobility was divided into rival factions and religious discord was rife, as the country split between adherents of the Roman Catholic faith and supporters of the new Protestant reforms. In his dealings with foreign powers, Henry had never achieved the military conquests of which he dreamed, merely making a few small gains in France, while his disastrous policy in Scotland had increased the threat of invasion from the north. Most dangerous of all, in terms of the future of his realm, Henry had not managed to achieve his aim of a secure succession. The 9-year-old Prince Edward had inherited an insolvent and insecure power base. For the next few years at least, the future looked distinctly bleak for the Tudor dynasty.

But was King Henry's reign really such a disaster? For more than four decades, he had held tenaciously on to power, surviving uprisings, invasion attempts and even excommunication to emerge as a proudly independent monarch, with considerably more power than his father had wielded. He had defied the power of the pope and the Holy Roman Emperor, bringing the English Church directly under his control. As head of the Church of England, he had purged it of many corrupt practices, and delivered the Bible in English to the ordinary people. He had also strengthened and enlarged the power of the monarchy, freeing it from the stranglehold of the clergy, incorporating Wales into the English kingdom, and even declaring his kingship over Ireland. Throughout his reign, King Henry had cut an imposing figure in Europe, making his small kingdom both feared and respected abroad. Even though his military gains were few, he had led his army with style, achieving more military victories than his fellow European rulers.

Henry's legacy to his country included many magnificent buildings. Christ Church College, Oxford, King's College Chapel, Cambridge, and Hampton Court Palace were all completed by him (although none of them was started by Henry VIII). Under the threat of invasion from France, Henry commissioned a string of imposing forts, and built the English navy into an impressive fighting force. Thanks largely to the efforts of Thomas Cromwell, the machinery of government became much more efficient in Henry's reign, as the courts of justice were reformed and the taxation system was made much fairer.

And yet the fact remains that King Henry squandered many opportunities. He had inherited a fortune from his father, but had exhausted it within the first two decades of his reign. Even more astoundingly, the vast sums of money gained for the royal exchequer by claiming monastic lands were frittered away in bouts of extravagance and military adventurism. In order to finance his French campaign of the 1540s, Henry sold off most of the lands that he had claimed from the abbeys. He also borrowed around £100,000 on foreign markets, leaving the debt for his successors to repay. Most disturbing of all, Henry twice devalued the English currency, calling in all the country's silver coins and reissuing them with a lower content of precious metal. These desperate measures produced short-term gains (providing Henry with around a third of a million pounds), but they had serious consequences for his country. Following the king's devaluations, economic activity slowed right down as people decided to spend their money rather than investing it in businesses.

Henry was profligate and self-indulgent, but monarchs of his period were expected to live splendidly. It can even be argued that he increased his country's standing abroad by such extravagant displays as the Field of the Cloth of Gold. However, he neglected his country's commercial interests by failing to encourage and support English trade as his father had done. During Henry's reign, foreign exploration was also abandoned and the momentum established by Henry VII was lost. At a time when valuable trading relations were being established, England was not even in the race. Henry failed to secure a share of the fabulous wealth from the New World that was filling the coffers of Portugal and Spain.

Perhaps the most serious criticism that can be levelled against King Henry VIII concerns his failure to care for his poorest subjects. In fact, the lot of the poor worsened during his reign, as the dissolution of the monasteries led to the loss of hundreds of schools, alms houses and hospitals that had previously been run by monks and nuns. The absence of these provisions was felt acutely by the poor, but with no channels for effective protest, it was left to the men of conscience, such as Sir Thomas More, to speak up about their plight. By the end of Henry's reign there was a growing groundswell of discontent, expressed chiefly through the medium of printed broadsheets and sermons. In particular, Henry's critics complained that the king's religious reforms had made life worse for his subjects. In the passionate words of one broadside author, the poor had been 'failed of their expectation and are now in more penury than ever they were ... Then they had hospitals and almshouses to be lodged in, but now they lie and starve in the streets.'

By the time of King Henry's death in 1547, the people of England were more than ready for a change. But they waited nervously to see what the future would bring. There were challenging times ahead for the Tudors.

Chapter 5
THE BOY KING AND THE NINE DAYS' QUEEN – EDWARD AND JANE

As King Henry VIII lay dying, his courtiers gathered around his bedside to pay their last respects. For nearly forty years, Henry had ruled with an iron will, but now England faced an uncertain future. What would become of Prince Edward, Henry's 9-year-old heir, and who would take charge of the country until he came of age? Would the English Church continue on its path of independence from Rome, and what would be the fate of Henry's daughters, Mary and Elizabeth? All of these questions must have been whispered in the corridors of the royal palace. Only one thing was certain – the next few years would not be easy ones for the Tudor family.

Taking Control

In his final days, King Henry made a last, desperate bid to exert control, signing a will that spelled out precisely how his kingdom should be ruled after his death. He would be succeeded as king by Prince Edward, who would be governed by a Council of the Regency – a body of 16 'entirely beloved' men with no single person in overall control. Henry's aim was to maintain the balance of power at court, a feat that he had managed brilliantly during his reign. But the king's dying wishes held no force in law. Within hours of Henry's death, a group of ambitious courtiers had taken matters into their own hands.

The dominant figure at court was Edward Seymour, brother of Jane Seymour, King Henry's third wife. As Prince Edward's uncle and England's most distinguished military commander, Seymour saw himself as the natural candidate to be the prince's guardian – and he lost no time in taking charge of the situation. As soon as he learned that the king was dead, Seymour set off to collect Prince Edward, who was staying in the country just outside London. Then he rode with Edward to Enfield Palace, a few miles north of London, where the young prince joined his 13-year-old sister, Elizabeth. Only when the two children were together did Seymour break the news of their father's death, dropping onto one knee in front of his new king. Apparently, the children sobbed so piteously that their servants were soon crying too. Eventually, however, they calmed themselves and Seymour prepared the king for his momentous ride to London.

On 31 January 1547, Henry's death was announced to Parliament (three days after the event) and Edward was proclaimed as Henry's heir. The new king was greeted by a deafening salute of cannon fire as he entered the Tower of London, where his royal councillors were waiting to pay humble homage to him. Later that day, Edward signed his approval of Seymour's appointment as Lord Protector of England and Governor of the King's Person. The stage was set for the Lord Protector to take control.

'A Young King Solomon'

Edward was crowned King of England and Ireland in Westminster Abbey on 20 February. On the eve of his coronation, the new king rode through the streets of

London on a magnificent horse caparisoned in scarlet. The pale young boy with golden-red hair was dressed in robes of silver embroidered with gold, and wore a cap and belt encrusted with rubies, pearls and diamonds. Lavish pageants were staged for the king's amusement, including a performance by a Spanish tightrope walker in St Paul's churchyard. The entertainer wriggled along the rope on his chest, causing Edward – in the words of one spectator – to 'laugh right heartily'. This charming image of Edward having fun is the last glimpse we have of him as a carefree child. From then on, the face that Edward presented to the world was solemn, reserved and dignified – and every inch a king.

As he emerged from the long ceremony of his coronation, King Edward was greeted ecstatically by his subjects. Here was a young King Solomon, they said, come to rule them wisely and well. As one observer wrote, 'How happy are we Englishmen of such a king, in whose childhood appeareth as perfect, grave virtue, godly zeal, desire of literature, gravity, prudence, justice and magnanimity as has heretofore been found in kings of most mature age.'

King Edward VI, it seemed, was a paragon. But what was the boy who wore the crown really like?

'This whole realm's most precious jewel'

From the moment of his birth, on 12 October 1537, King Henry VIII's son was a celebrity. After 28 years of waiting for a royal heir, Prince Edward's birth was greeted with extravagant celebrations, which were only marred by the news of Queen Jane's tragic death, just twelve days after her son's birth. To his proud father, the infant Edward was 'This whole realm's most precious jewel' and no expense was spared in his care. The rooms of his princely apartments were decorated with priceless tapestries, and his clothes, books and cutlery were encrusted with gold and precious jewels. In an age when everyone lived in terror of sudden death, fanatical care was taken over Edward's health and safety: the floors of his chambers were washed three times a day and his food was prepared from only the finest of ingredients.

The prince's early years were spent in the care of a select group of gentlewomen, who supervised his daily routine, teaching him elegant manners and basic reading and writing skills. At the age of 6, however, Edward moved into a world of men and his education began in earnest. Chief among Edward's tutors were Richard Cox, later bishop of Ely, and Dr John Cheke from Cambridge – both outstanding scholars with Protestant inclinations. From them, Edward received a thorough grounding in Latin and Greek, scripture, history and geography. There were also lessons in French, German, Italian and handwriting, while William Thomas, clerk to the King's council, coached the prince in politics and statesmanship. Physical sports befitting a king were not neglected either, with lessons in fencing, horsemanship and the rules of hunting, and Edward became proficient at playing the lute.

Edward's education did not take place in isolation,

as the king assembled fourteen sons of nobles to be schooled alongside his son. Apparently Edward's favourite among his schoolfellows was the Irish-born Barnaby FitzPatrick, and when he became king, FitzPatrick was given the dubious honour of being the royal whipping boy, receiving any beatings that Edward earned. Prince Edward also shared some of his lessons with Elizabeth, revelling in the challenge of keeping up with his clever older sister.

By all accounts, Edward was a star pupil. At the age of 7 he was already expert at conjugating Latin verbs and could compose his own verses in Latin. When Elizabeth's tutor Roger Ascham visited the 12-year-old king, he reported that Edward was 'wonderfully in advance of his years'. Studying and reading were Edward's natural pastimes, although he happily took part in games and races with his fellow pupils. Unlike his sister Elizabeth, he did not inherit his father's passion for hunting or music and he positively disapproved of dancing. When he was just 8 years old, Edward sent a letter to his stepmother, Catherine Parr, asking her to remind his sister Mary (then aged 29) that she was ruining her reputation by her love of 'foreign dances and other merriments that do not become a most Christian princess'. It is not recorded whether Queen Catherine judged it wise to pass on this priggish piece of advice to Mary.

Above all, Edward's passion was religion. From an early age he loved to read the Bible, and developed a taste for long, complex sermons, taking detailed notes about the preachers' arguments. By the time of his coronation, Edward already had the makings of a fanatical Protestant and, at the age of 12, he wrote a treatise attacking the pope as the Antichrist.

What Edward clearly lacked was a mother's love. His father was a distant and rather frightening figure – although he would occasionally indulge in a boisterous romp with his son – and his first two stepmothers, Anne of Cleves and Catherine Howard, took little notice of him. Only when King Henry married Catherine Parr did

Edward receive any real maternal affection. Catherine welcomed him into the royal household and the 5-year-old Edward responded eagerly, addressing her as 'my most dear mother'. A letter survives from Edward, then aged 8, in which he expresses his gratitude to Catherine, saying that 'I received so many benefits from you that my mind can hardly grasp.'

Thanks to Catherine's efforts, Edward had the chance to spend more time with his sisters, Mary and Elizabeth. Mary was twenty-one years older than Edward, and did not share her brother's Protestant convictions, having been brought up as a devout Catholic by her mother, Catherine of Aragon. But she was still devoted to the solemn boy, showering him with gifts and affection. In return, young Edward sent Mary gifts and letters, composed in Latin, in which he told her that he loved her more than anyone else. In Elizabeth – just four years older than him – Edward had a close companion. Elizabeth and Edward were both precociously clever. They also shared an emotional bond, having lost their mothers when they were infants. Surviving letters between the pair reveal how they hated to be parted and looked forward keenly to their times together. In 1546, Edward wrote fondly to Elizabeth, 'Change of place did not vex me so much, dearest sister, as your going from me... It is some comfort in my grief that my chamberlain tells me I may hope to visit you soon.'

For almost four years, from the time of Henry's last marriage until his death, Edward enjoyed a glimpse of what family life might mean (albeit a very formal and privileged one), but all this disappeared on the day that he became King Edward VI.

The Rule of the Lord Protector

The reign of Edward VI began with the young king firmly under his uncle's thumb. The Lord Protector, Edward Seymour, was a serious-minded man with a strong desire to improve the condition of the poor, but his unshakeable sense that he was always right made him many enemies. His method of dealing with the king was to keep him chronically short of money and to ban any pursuits that might tempt a young boy into frivolity or extravagance. In the meantime, Seymour got on with the business of governing England, with very little recourse to the advice of either the Royal Council or Parliament.

The Lord Protector faced some serious challenges. King Henry had left the crown desperately short of funds. The kingdom was divided over religion, with some extreme Protestants pushing for radical reforms while many people still clung obstinately to their Catholic traditions. Henry's policy of dissolving the monasteries had left no provisions for care of the poor and the sick. There was also widespread social unrest as landowners embarked on a policy of enclosure – taking over the common grazing grounds for their own use. In addition to these domestic problems, there was the constant fear that the Catholic rulers of Europe could move to supplant the young Protestant king with a Catholic monarch – in the person of his older sister Mary.

Perhaps the most pressing problem facing Edward Seymour was hostility from Scotland. There had been trouble with the Scots ever since the early 1540s when King Henry VIII had proposed that Prince Edward should be betrothed to the infant Mary, Queen of Scots. Through this proposal, Henry had hoped to gain control of Scotland, but many Scots believed that Mary should be promised to the son of the French king instead. In 1544 the Scottish Parliament refused to sign the marriage agreement, otherwise known as the Treaty of Greenwich, and Henry launched a crushing attack on Edinburgh. The following year a Scottish counter-attack ended in victory for the Scots at the Battle of Ancrum Moor. This violent struggle for power between the Scots and the English would later be known as 'the rough wooing', and was still raging when Edward came to the throne.

In 1547 Seymour masterminded a crushing victory at the Battle of Pinkie Cleugh, and went on to establish a network of garrisons in Scotland. For a few months, the

English managed to resist all Scottish attacks, but their fortunes changed when the Scots formed an alliance with the French. By the summer of 1548 the French king was sending reinforcements to Scotland for the defence of Edinburgh, and in the following year Seymour was forced to withdraw from Scotland, crippled by the cost of maintaining his Scottish defences. By this time, Mary, Queen of Scots had moved to France, where she was promised in marriage to the dauphin, the heir to the French throne.

There was also trouble closer to home. By 1548 resentment at the enclosures was mounting and there were rumours that a rebellion was brewing. Seymour responded by setting up a series of commissions to investigate grievances about the loss of common land. This policy gained Seymour popular support, earning him the nickname of the 'good duke', but it failed to address the root of the problem. In 1549 a Norfolk tanner named Robert Kett led a popular uprising in protest against the greed of the landowners. Kett gathered a force of some 15,000 men, and stormed the city of Norwich, causing great alarm to the Lord Protector. When an initial force of 1,500 failed to subdue the rebellion, Seymour sent John Dudley to Norfolk with an army of around 14,000 men. Dudley's efficient suppression of Kett's rebellion marked the start of his unstoppable rise to power.

While Seymour was kept busy with problems at home and abroad, he was also actively pursuing a campaign of religious reform. With the support of Archbishop Thomas Cranmer, Seymour authorized the dissolution of chantry chapels – special chapels established to celebrate sung Masses, usually for the soul of a deceased wealthy donor. Chapels were ransacked throughout the land and stripped of their treasures, with the proceeds being claimed for the crown and the nobility. Seymour's campaign was clearly underpinned by financial motives – the chapels provided a valuable source of revenue – but Cranmer's views on Chantry chapels were devoutly held. As

Archbishop of Canterbury, he saw it as his duty to rid the English Church of the corrupt practices of Rome. In 1549, Cranmer composed the *Book of Common Prayer*, written in English, and detailing all the prayers and services to be held in English places of worship. In the same year the Act of Uniformity decreed that these new services should be made compulsory, replacing the Latin Mass. The Act was met with strong opposition at all levels of society. Two protesting bishops – Stephen Gardiner and Edmund Bonner – were both imprisoned in the Tower of London, while a people's uprising in Devon and Cornwall, known as the Prayer Book Rebellion, had to be put down by force.

Thomas Seymour's bids for power

Edward Seymour was never truly secure in his role as Lord Protector. There were plenty of men at court eager to challenge his right to dominate the young king and the most dangerous of all was his younger brother, Thomas Seymour. Thomas was handsome, dashing and flamboyant. He was also prepared to play some very dangerous games in his struggle to gain control over the king. By bribing John Fowler, one of Edward's servants, he managed to smuggle gifts of money to his royal nephew. Thomas hoped that these gifts would win Edward's favour, but the king remained loyal to the Lord Protector, refusing to sign a document agreeing to a joint protectorate by both his uncles.

Thomas Seymour was also exploring other means to pursue his ambition. In 1547, he married King Henry's widow, Catherine Parr, acquiring great wealth and prestige, and also gaining access to the 13-year-old Elizabeth, who was staying in Catherine's Chelsea home. Thomas used his boisterous charms to tease and excite Elizabeth, until Catherine sent her away to protect her reputation. However, following Catherine's death in 1548, Thomas once again turned his attentions towards Elizabeth.

Thomas Seymour's most desperate bid for power came in January 1549, when he attempted to kidnap

King Edward. Using a duplicate key, Thomas entered the king's apartments at Hampton Court accompanied by a small party of armed men. He proceeded to unlock Edward's bedroom door, where he was confronted by the king's spaniel. Faced with a wildly barking dog, Thomas drew his handgun and shot it dead, terrifying Edward and alerting the guard. The incident was reported to the Royal Council, who committed Thomas to the Tower. At his subsequent trial, Thomas' many schemes were exposed and he was beheaded for treason.

The Fall of the Lord Protector

The other major thorn in the Lord Protector's side was John Dudley, Earl of Warwick. The son of Edmund Dudley, King Henry VII's hated tax collector, he had served as Lord Admiral for Henry VIII, and had proved his worth in Edward's reign by quashing Kett's Rebellion in Norfolk. Dudley was greedy, unscrupulous and scheming and, by 1549, he was hungry for power.

Henry Tudor and Elizabeth of York had a marriage of convenience, but their union turned out to be unusually close and loving. Henry VII was the only Tudor who managed to have a long-term, stable family life.

Compared with his predecessors and descendants, Henry seems to have been obsessed with making money. Some contemporary writers depicted the king as a heartless miser, bleeding his people dry and even allowing Catherine of Aragon to starve.

The historic meeting of Henry and Francis at the Field of the Cloth of Gold symbolized a new era of friendship and peace between their nations. But it was not to last.

During the fourteen years that he worked for Henry, Thomas Wolsey had more power than any royal adviser had ever enjoyed before. However, his loyalty to the pope proved to be his downfall.

NNO · ETATIS · · SVÆ · XLIX

An imposing portrait of Henry VIII, painted when the king was around 50 years old. Henry deteriorated fast in the next five years. In his final months, he suffered terrifying fits when he turned black in the face and struggled to breathe.

Catherine of Aragon

Anne Boleyn

Jane Seymour

Anne of Cleves

Catherine Howard

Catherine Parr

In this allegorical painting of Edward VI's religious reformation, the king is shown overcoming the pope and his Catholic priests.

The Execution of Lady Jane Grey, *engraved from a painting by Paul Delaroche.*

*On 3 August 1553 Mary I arrived in London to claim the
English crown. She was greeted by cheering crowds, and people
of all classes pledged their allegiance to her.*

Queen Elizabeth in her coronation robes, painted by an unknown Tudor artist. At just 25 years old, the slender young queen must have been a very striking sight.

The Spanish Armada consisted of 130 ships, carrying over 25,000 men. It must have presented a terrifying sight as it sailed into the English Channel.

The Armada Portrait *was painted by George Gower to commemorate the English victory in 1588.*

Edward the Victim?

Edward rarely revealed his feelings, but one incident provides an intriguing insight into his emotional state. Reginald Pole, later Archbishop of Canterbury, related that the king once seized on a falcon perched in his bedchamber. In a cruel rage, Edward slowly plucked out all the bird's feathers before deliberately ripping it into pieces, saying as he did so that 'he likened himself to the falcon, whom everybody plucked, but that he would pluck them hereafter and tear them into four parts'. This disturbing act appears to be a rare expression of anger by a boy who felt himself to be constantly manipulated by those around him.

Railing at the incompetence of the Lord Protector, he gathered a group of supporters in the Royal Council, and prepared for a coup.

In early October, a nervous Edward Seymour took possession of the king, and barricaded himself in Windsor Castle, from where Edward wrote miserably, 'Methinks I am in prison.' However, Seymour's stand was to prove short-lived, and within a week he was arrested and held in the Tower. The charges against the Lord Protector were, in King Edward's words: 'ambition, vainglory, entering into rash wars ...[and]... enriching himself of my treasure'. But he was soon released in response to a public outcry against the mistreatment of the 'good duke'. Seymour was even restored to the Royal Council, but by that time control had passed to John Dudley. In 1552, Dudley finally managed to dispose of his rival, arresting Seymour for scheming to overthrow him. Seymour was beheaded in January 1522. Edward noted his uncle's death in his *Chronicle*, simply noting 'the duke of Somerset had his head cut off upon Tower Green between eight and nine o'clock in the morning.'

The Rule of the Lord President

In October 1549, John Dudley assumed the title of Lord President of the Royal Council, and prepared to work his charms on the king. By now the 12-year-old

Edward was taking a keen interest in the affairs of his realm – and Dudley knew just how to flatter and influence him. Relaxing the strict regime imposed by Edward's uncle, he laid on a succession of treats for the king, including spectacular military displays and water tournaments. At the same time, he began to consult Edward on matters of state, gradually increasing the scope of royal involvement. By the time Edward was 14 years old, he had his own Counsel for the Estate. The Counsel members were picked by the king and in their weekly meetings he could 'hear the debating of things of most importance'. It is not clear how much real power Edward wielded, but Dudley certainly managed to make him feel that he was at the heart of government.

Dudley's period in power was marked by decisive action on several fronts. In the field of foreign policy, he took a pragmatic approach. Recognizing that England could not afford to be at war, he ceased all hostilities with Scotland and France, signing a peace treaty with the French that agreed to the English withdrawal from Boulogne and the recall of all garrisons from Scotland. At home, he introduced measures to prevent local unrest, installing lord lieutenants in the regions with orders to report any trouble to the Royal Council. Dudley also tackled the depleted state of the kingdom's finances, restoring confidence in the English coinage, which had been falling steeply as rumours grew that the country was slipping into chaos, and he initiated a thorough review of tax collection methods, cracking down on embezzlement of government funds.

With the king's full support, Dudley pushed forward an ever more radical programme of religious reform. Priests were given orders to get rid of all 'idolatrous images and superstitious books', clergy were no longer required to be celibate and the Catholic Mass was effectively abolished – replaced by a revised version of Cranmer's *Book of Common Prayer*. By the end of Edward's reign, the English Church was unequivocally Protestant in character.

Edward's Illness

By the spring of 1552, Edward was 14 years old and desperate to assume more power. He had persuaded his advisers that he could accede to the throne at the age of 16, rather than 18, but his 16th birthday was still two years away and he was bursting with plans for his realm. One of the measures he was keen to introduce was the setting up of charitable institutions for the poor, and in February he established two foundations – a hospital for the sick in the priory of St Thomas', Southwark, and a school for the children of the poor, named Christ's Hospital.

Then, in early April, Edward suffered an attack of measles, which may have been combined with smallpox. At first he appeared to make a full recovery, taking part in a series of ceremonies and entertainments, before setting out on a royal progress in June. The king's advisers had organized a hectic schedule through the south-west of the country, combining official duties with banquets and hunts, and by August Edward was exhausted.

According to one commentator, 'It was observed on all sides how sickly he looked, and general pity was felt for him by the people.' In mid-September, the king was at last persuaded to return to Windsor where a doctor diagnosed tuberculosis, a disease of the lungs for which there was no known cure. Powerless to help his royal patient, the doctor simply recommended that the king should rest.

Over the next few months, the king's condition grew steadily worse. By his 15th birthday in October he was coughing blood, and by Christmas he was wracked by violent bouts of fever. Dudley was desperately worried for his future. He recognized that Edward's death would bring the Catholic Mary to the throne, with dire consequences for Protestants, but he resolved to act as if there was nothing wrong, and the Christmas festivities went ahead as usual. By February, however, rumours of Edward's illness were spreading and his sister Mary resolved to visit her brother. Mary was shocked to see how much Edward had changed, but he reassured her that he was on the mend. On 21 February, he was strong enough to open a new session of Parliament. After Parliament rose, Edward left for Greenwich, where he confidently expected that a few weeks' rest would restore him to health.

King Henry's Will

King Henry VIII's final Act of Succession stated that his only son, Edward, would succeed to the English throne. In the case of Edward dying without any heirs, the throne would pass to Mary, and, if she died childless, to Elizabeth. If Elizabeth's line also died out, Henry decreed that the crown should pass to the heirs of his younger sister, Mary. (Henry's older sister Margaret had married the King of Scotland, an old enemy of England, so her heirs were ruled out of his will.) Mary's eldest granddaughter was Lady Jane Grey, and in 1553 she became England's 'nine days' queen'.

It was not to be. At the end of April, the German ambassador reported to the Emperor, 'I hear from a trustworthy source that the King is undoubtedly becoming weaker as time passes, and wasting away. The matter he ejects from his mouth is sometimes coloured greenish-yellow and black, sometimes pink like the colour of blood.' By this time, Edward's body was covered with painful ulcers and his legs had become so swollen that he was forced to stay lying on his back. One royal physician predicted that the king would be dead by June, but Dudley continued to issue reassuring bulletins about Edward's health.

A Question of Succession

Dudley was playing a desperate game to try to guarantee his personal survival. If Mary or Elizabeth were to succeed to the throne, his power would be destroyed, and he might even face imprisonment and death. But if he could persuade the king to nominate a candidate of his choice, he might remain the power behind the throne.

Dudley's candidate for the English throne was Lady Jane Grey, King Henry VIII's great niece and Edward's cousin once removed. Lady Jane's mother was the daughter of Princess Mary, the younger sister of Henry VIII, and she had been mentioned in his will as being fourth in line to the throne, after Edward, Mary and Elizabeth. Jane was a quiet, studious girl, who, like Edward, was a fanatical Protestant. She was also only 15 years old and firmly in the power of John Dudley. On 25 May 1553, Jane had married his son, Guildford Dudley, and John was confident that he could compel his new daughter-in-law to do his wishes.

With this aim in mind, Dudley began to work on the king, but he needed time to make sure that all his schemes were in place. What if the king should die before all the necessary arrangements were made? With callous disregard for Edward's welfare, Dudley dismissed his doctors and employed a female quack, who undertook to dose her patient with an arsenic mixture that would keep him alive long enough for

Dudley to complete his machinations.

As Edward swallowed his terrible medicine, Dudley extracted royal approval for his plans. Confronted with the prospect of his kingdom returning to the Catholic faith, it was not difficult for Edward to be persuaded to exclude his sister Mary from the succession. But turning Edward against Elizabeth was a harder task. Dudley asserted that Mary could not be 'put by unless the Lady Elizabeth were put by too' and he warned Edward of the dangers to his realm if either of his sisters were to marry a Catholic prince. He also reminded Edward that both his sisters were still officially bastards (Henry had never revoked the act of Parliament by which they were declared illegitimate) and he sang the praises of Lady Jane Grey who was legitimate, a fervent Protestant, and already safely married.

Dudley argued well, and Edward was convinced. Summoning all his remaining strength, he commanded Dudley to draw up a will entitled 'My Devise for the Succession', which he copied out with a trembling hand.

The final document invested the crown in 'Lady Jane and her heirs males' and after them to Jane's sisters and their heirs. Edward's own sisters were described as 'illegitimate and not lawfully begotten' and so 'disabled to claim the said imperial crown'.

Dudley had his 'Devise', but he still needed the approval of the country's leading judges. The judges were duly summoned to the king's bedchamber, where they protested that Edward was still a minor and had no legal right to contradict his father's will. Dudley faced an impasse, until the king himself intervened, commanding the judges' obedience 'with sharp words and angry countenance'. Faced with the wrath of the dying king, the judges capitulated and granted their approval. Edward's Devise was duly signed by over a hundred councillors, nobles, archbishop and bishops, many of whom would later claim that they had been coerced or bribed by Dudley.

Medicine in Tudor Times

Tudor medicine was a very inexact science. Physicians still followed the teachings of Aristotle, believing that the body was governed by four humours – blood, phlegm, yellow bile and black bile. It was widely maintained that illness was caused by an excess of one of the humours and it was the doctor's job to restore the balance of humours in their patient's body. Cures were achieved by bleeding, purging with laxatives, the use of emetics and dosing with medicines. These medicines were concocted from a mixture of herbs, but often included animal parts and ground-up minerals.

Bleeding was a very common practice, as many illnesses were attributed to the problem of too much blood in the body. Some doctors used leeches to suck a patient's blood. Others cut a vein and used a bowl to collect the blood. Physicians also practised cupping, applying a special cup to the patient's skin. The cup had previously been warmed up and as its surface cooled, the air inside it also cooled, contracted and pulled on the skin so hard that blood came to the surface.

Operations were carried out by surgeons, using knives and saws. But without the availability of either anaesthetics or antiseptics, operations were excruciatingly painful and dangerous for the patient. Wounds often became poisoned through infection, leading ultimately to the patient's death. Minor operations were performed by barber-surgeons, who advertised their services with a red and white striped pole, representing blood and bandages.

Only the wealthy could afford to consult a doctor. In towns, people visited apothecaries who supplied them with medicines. In villages, a local 'wise woman' concocted cures. Tudor cures generally relied on a mixture of herbs and magic. A popular cure for gout was an ointment made from worms, the marrow from pigs' bones and a mixture of herbs, all boiled together with the corpse of a red-haired dog. Headaches were treated with a medicine made from lavender, sage, marjoram and roses, but it was also believed that a headache would be banished if a patient pressed a hangman's rope to his head. For cases of smallpox, red curtains were hung around the sickbed in the belief that the red light could cure the patient.

Edward's Last Days

By the end of June, Edward was suffering agonies of arsenic poisoning. His body had swollen up like a balloon, his skin had started to turn black and his fingers and toes were being eaten away by gangrene. Every breath caused him pain and he could hardly speak. Dudley no longer needed to keep the king alive, so he dismissed the female quack and recalled the royal doctors. Faced with a patient who was clearly dying, they concocted various brews, one of which included spearmint, fennel, liverwort, turnip, dates, raisins, mace, celery and pork from a nine-day-old sow. When the courtier and statesman William Cecil was told what the medicine contained, he retorted, 'God deliver us from the physicians!'

As June turned into July, it was clear that the king could not last much longer. His breathing was desperately laboured and he lay in a feverish delirium. Finally, in the early evening of 6 July, Edward whispered a final prayer, committing his soul into God's care and begging God to 'defend this realm from papistry and maintain Thy true religion'. Edward's short but eventful reign had come to an end.

Lady Jane

While the king lay dying, Dudley's wife, the Duchess of Somerset, paid a visit to Lady Jane Grey, her new daughter-in-law. The duchess came bearing some surprising news. 'If God should call the King to His mercy,' she is reported to have said, 'it will be needful for you to go immediately to the Tower. His Majesty hath made you heir to his realm.' Later, Jane recorded that she was 'greatly disturbed' by her mother-in-law's news, and 'could make little account of these words'. She had only a few days to ponder her situation before she became an unwilling pawn in some very dangerous games.

As the eldest daughter of King Henry's niece, Lady Frances Grey, Jane had grown up on the edge of the royal family. Her father, Henry Grey, was a courtier in the royal household, and her family had a grand house in London, as well as a dilapidated country seat. Jane's parents, who held the title of Duke and Duchess of Suffolk, were a ruthlessly ambitious pair, who had been scheming ever since Jane's birth for her to make a brilliant marriage, and their dearest wish was that their daughter would be King Edward's wife.

In preparation for a distinguished future, Jane was given an excellent education. When she was only 4, the Suffolks appointed a young Cambridge scholar to be her first tutor, and, at the age of 6, the little girl embarked on a strict study regime, learning Latin and Greek, French, Spanish and Italian, as well as the skills of handwriting, dancing and needlework.

Jane was an excellent pupil, but she failed to please her parents. They were disappointed in their daughter's looks – she was small and thin, with a pleasant, freckled face and sandy-coloured hair – and she hated grand clothes, preferring to dress modestly in black and white. They also felt affronted by Jane's failure to enjoy the sporty, outdoor life. At the end of a hard day's studying, an exhausted Jane would be forced to go hunting and hawking with her parents. If she dared to object, she would be in trouble. In fact, the young Jane spent most of her childhood in trouble, as she later revealed to Roger Ascham, 'For when I am in the presence of either Father or Mother, whether I speak, keep silence, sit, stand or go, eat, drink, be merry or sad, be sewing, playing, dancing, or doing anything else, I must do it as it were in such weight, measure and number, even so perfectly as God made the world; or else I am so sharply taunted, so cruelly threatened, yes presently sometimes with pinches, nips and bobs and other ways ... that I think myself in hell.'

It must have come as a great relief to Jane when, at the age of 9, she was sent to live in the London household of Catherine Parr, widow of King Henry. The king's daughter Elizabeth (then aged 13) was also living with Catherine, and the two girls shared their lessons, becoming close friends. Lady Jane's parents clearly saw her move into Catherine's household as a chance for their daughter to spend more time with the young king, but in fact Edward and Jane rarely met. On the rare occasions when they were together, Lady Jane approached the king with the utmost respect, curtseying three times when she entered his presence and kneeling humbly as they talked.

Lady Jane's parents were not the only ones to have plans for her. Around the time that Jane arrived in London, Catherine Parr married Thomas Seymour, brother of the Lord Protector, and Jane became his ward. Seymour saw Jane as a useful tool in his schemes to gain more power over the king and he began to plot for Jane to marry Edward. All his plans came to nothing, however, and in February 1549 Seymour was arrested and tried for treason.

Following Thomas Seymour's arrest, Jane returned to her parents' London home. During her time away she had experienced some very hard knocks. In the spring of 1548 Elizabeth had been sent away, after it was discovered that Seymour was flirting immodestly with her. A few months later Catherine Parr had died, leaving the 10-year-old Jane in the care of the unscrupulous Thomas Seymour. For the next six months, until

Seymour's arrest, Jane was in the uncomfortable position of being in the protection of a notorious womanizer, who was determined to use her in his bid for power.

Once it was clear that Thomas Seymour's plans had failed, the Suffolks lost no time in arranging a new match for their daughter. Jane was betrothed to marry young Edward Seymour, the son of the Lord Protector – at least until a greater prize came into view. Meanwhile, Lady Jane pursued her studies. By the time she entered her teens, it was clear that she was a remarkably able young woman. During her period as a companion to Elizabeth, she had come into contact with some eminent scholars, and she was renowned for her erudition. By the time she was 15, Jane was completely fluent in Latin and Greek and had embarked on a study of Hebrew in order to read the Scriptures in the original text. She had also become a committed Protestant.

What Jane longed for most of all was an uninterrupted life of study, but this was not to be. By January 1553, King Edward was dying and John Dudley was plotting to keep his hold on the throne. Dudley decided that his only hope for the future lay in Jane's coronation, and in order to gain control of the future queen, he proposed a marriage between Lady Jane and his son, Lord Guildford Dudley. Unsurprisingly, the ambitious Suffolks were eager to oblige the most powerful man in England and the wedding was swiftly arranged. Only Jane was unhappy with the arrangement, protesting that she was already engaged to be married, but she was swiftly subdued by a thorough whipping from her forceful mother. The marriage that took place on 25 May 1553 was an unashamedly political affair. Both sets of parents had previously agreed that the match should not be consummated, so that it could be annulled if Dudley's bid for power failed, and the newly married bride returned to her parents' home. With some relief, Jane resumed her studies, but within two months she had received the fateful message that she had been chosen to be the next queen.

'Jane the Quene'

Three days after Edward's death, Dudley sent his daughter to bring Lady Jane Grey to Syon House, the family's mansion on the River Thames. According to Jane's own account of her brief reign, she was then led into a grand chamber, filled with nobles, with a throne set on a dais at one end. Dudley solemnly announced the death of Edward VI, followed by the pronouncement that Lady Jane Grey was queen, and everyone knelt in homage while Jane collapsed in shock.

At first Jane refused to accept her new role, protesting that Lady Mary was the rightful heir, but after some harsh words from her parents and father-in-law, she capitulated and agreed to sit on the throne. A relieved Dudley led the company in swearing allegiance to their new queen, while Jane stayed silent, convinced in her heart that what she was doing was wrong.

On the following day, Queen Jane made her royal progress to the Tower of London, the traditional waiting place for monarchs awaiting coronation. Travelling by river, she set off early in a splendid barge, dressed in a green velvet robe embroidered with gold. As the barge moved slowly down the River Thames, royal heralds roamed the streets of London, proclaiming Jane as queen, only to be greeted by stunned disbelief. Even when Jane was welcomed into the Tower by rounds of cannon fire, there were few who gathered to cheer the new queen.

That evening, a grand banquet was held in Jane's honour, but the celebrations were overshadowed by the news that the Lady Mary was gathering support in East Anglia. Later the royal bedchamber was the scene of a furious row as Jane's husband, Lord Guildford Dudley, demanded the right to be crowned king. Jane adamantly refused to agree, causing Guildford to burst into tears and run off to find his mother, but even the protestations of her ferocious mother-in-law failed to make the young queen change her mind.

For the next few days, Jane settled into a new routine. In the mornings, the Royal Council met to decide the business of the day, with Lord Guildford presiding. This was followed by a formal dinner, in which the queen sat in state, flanked by her redoubtable mother and mother-in-law. In the afternoon Jane was informed of all the decisions that had been made in her name, signing all documents with her new signature 'Jane the Quene'. For the rest of the time, she stayed in her private apartments in the Tower, afraid that Dudley was plotting to poison her. But she had no idea just how insecure Dudley's position was.

Just two days into Queen Jane's reign, things were already looking bad for Dudley. Mary had gathered an army of 15,000 men at Framlingham Castle in Suffolk, and support for her cause was growing fast. In the eyes of many English people – both Protestants and Catholics – Mary was the rightful heir to the English throne. She was also held in great public affection. Many English people had fond memories of Mary's mother, Catherine of Aragon, and felt that the Lady Mary had been poorly treated for many years.

Aware of the growing mood in the country, Dudley

was reluctant to leave London. He doubted the loyalty of some of his supporters and feared that they would change sides once his back was turned. But he also knew that only he was qualified to lead the counterattack. Meanwhile, news kept arriving of new areas of the country that had declared allegiance to Mary.

On 14 July, Dudley rode out of London at the head of an army of around 5,000 men, announcing that he would bring back Mary captive or dead. But as soon as he left the Tower, many councillors slipped quietly away. At the same time, broadsheets supporting Mary's claim to the throne had begun to appear in the streets of London, and by the following day people were openly professing their loyalty to Queen Mary.

In the Tower, Queen Jane waited to hear from Dudley, but the news was bad. His troops were defecting fast and he was so clearly outnumbered that any armed confrontation could only end in defeat. In London, too, loyalties were shifting. By 18 July, only three council members were left in the Tower – the Duke of Suffolk

(Lady Jane Grey's father), Archbishop Cranmer (in his role as defender of the Protestant faith) and John Cheke (former tutor to King Edward), while a much larger group, led by the Earl of Arundel, had visited St Paul's Cathedral to give public thanks for the kingdom's delivery from Dudley's treachery.

On 19 July, Arundel ordered the Lord Mayor to proclaim Mary Queen of England – and London went wild. In the words of one commentator, 'All the citizens made great and many fires through all the streets and banqueting also, with all the bells ringing in every parish church, till ten of the clock at night.' Jane's short and unhappy reign had come to an end.

The End of Lady Jane

The celebrations were at their height when Lady Jane's father arrived in her chamber, where she sat under a canopy eating her supper. 'You are no longer queen,' he announced, as he began to rip down the canopy. 'You must put off your royal robes and be content with a private life.' His daughter's response was admirably calm. Stating that she was happy to take off her robes, she simply asked her father when she could go home. But she received no reply. He had already decided to switch allegiance to Mary and was abandoning his daughter to face her fate alone. Within a few hours, guards had arrived in the Tower to inform Jane, Guildford and his mother that they were all prisoners of the Crown.

The following day Dudley was arrested in Cambridge, and four days later he was paraded through London in front of an angry crowd howling for his death. Dudley was locked in the Tower, along with his sons and a number of councillors. Meanwhile, Lady Jane was moved into the house of the Gentleman Gaoler of the Tower, where she was allowed books and writing materials while she waited to hear what would become of her.

At first the news was encouraging. In an audience with Lady Jane Grey's mother, Queen Mary promised that neither Jane nor her parents would be harmed. But while Jane's parents were soon safely back at home, she remained in the Tower, and the Greys made no more efforts to help their daughter. Meanwhile, Mary announced her intention of keeping Jane and her husband in custody until it was safe to pardon and release them. Secure in the belief that she would soon be free, Jane returned to her studies, penning – rather unwisely – some passionate attacks on the Catholic faith.

On 23 August Dudley was tried, found guilty and executed. By this time Jane had been allowed a little more freedom, and had begun to take walks along the battlements and to dine with the gaoler and his wife. Then, in November, Jane, Lord Guildford Dudley and Archbishop Cranmer faced trial for high treason. All three were found guilty and condemned to death, but Mary had resolved to be merciful and the prisoners remained in the Tower, awaiting the time when the queen would grant them her pardon.

Mary's intention was to delay Jane's pardon and release until she herself had married and produced an heir. But things did not turn out to be straightforward

for the queen. Mary's plans to marry Prince Philip of
Spain alienated many of her people, who hated the idea
that their country might be ruled by a foreign, Catholic
monarch. In such an atmosphere of hostility, it was clear
that Lady Jane could become a focus for rebellion and
Mary tightened security at the Tower, banning Jane's
walks in the gardens. Then, in January 1554, Mary's
spies uncovered a planned rebellion against the queen.
The rebellion was led by a leading Protestant noble, Sir
Thomas Wyatt, and Jane's father was involved. Once the
conspirators were rounded up, Mary's council pressed
for her to rid herself of anyone who could provide a
focus for future unrest, and the queen reluctantly agreed.

On the evening of 7 February, Lady Jane Grey was
told to prepare for death. The date of her execution was
two days away, but first Mary offered Jane the chance
of a reprieve if she would convert to the Catholic faith.
Mary sent a kindly counsellor, Richard of Feckenham,
Abbot of Westminster, to talk and pray with Jane, but
she remained adamant in her Protestant convictions,

although she did agree that the abbot could be present at her death.

At ten o'clock on the morning of 12 February 1554, Lady Jane walked the short distance to Tower Green, sombrely dressed in black and reading her prayer book. Then she recited a psalm, before being blindfolded and kneeling in front of the execution block. For a brief moment she panicked when she couldn't find the block, but her hands were guided and she laid down her head calmly for the executioner to do his deed.

Later that day, Jane's body was laid to rest in a chapel on the north side of Tower Green between Anne Boleyn and Catherine Howard. Nearby lay the remains of Seymour and Dudley, the men who had dominated Edward VI's short reign. With the death of the Nine Days' Queen, a short but dramatic episode in the history of the Tudors had come to an end.

Chapter 6
BLOODY MARY – THE LIFE AND REIGN OF MARY I

When she came to the throne, in 1553, Mary Tudor was welcomed ecstatically by the English crowds. A mere five years later, she was widely hated and feared. In her short and violent reign, almost 300 people were burned at the stake in the name of religion. Yet the woman who came to be known as 'Bloody Mary' had only ever sought to do the best for her subjects.

The enigma of Mary's character has never been entirely explained, but its roots must lie in her extraordinary and troubled childhood.

'The greatest pearl in the kingdom'

Princess Mary was born on 18 February 1516 at Greenwich Palace, the daughter of Queen Catherine of Aragon and King Henry VIII. She was not her parents' first child; the queen had already lost three sons and a daughter – all either stillborn or dying soon after birth – and the royal couple must have waited with trepidation to see if their precious daughter would survive. As a princess of the realm, Mary was welcomed into the world with a splendid christening ceremony in the friars' church near the royal palace, and furnished with her own set of royal apartments, presided over by a large company of gentlewomen and servants, all dressed in Mary's livery of blue and green.

To Mary's proud father, his daughter was 'the greatest pearl in the kingdom', but that did not mean that he spent much time with her. For the first few years of her life, Princess Mary would only have seen her parents on special occasions, when she was presented to them in her finest clothes. Henry liked to carry the infant Mary around the room, before swiftly returning her to her gentlewomen, and it was his proud boast that his pretty daughter 'never cried'.

King Henry was soon to put his 'pearl' to diplomatic use. When Mary was just 2 years old, a 'treaty of universal peace' was concluded with France and sealed by the betrothal of Princess Mary to the dauphin. Throughout the long ceremony, the infant princess was held in the arms of her nurse, and she was even presented with a diamond ring to fit her tiny finger. The French marriage contract lasted only four years before diplomatic relations with France changed, and Mary was promised instead to her mother's cousin, the 22-year-old Holy Roman Emperor, Charles V. This time the 6-year-old Mary performed in front of the emperor's ambassador, dancing elegantly and playing the virginals, and a glowing report was sent back to Charles. The little princess was touchingly attached to her future husband, sending him numerous gifts and letters of affection. The union between Charles and Mary never took place (in fact, in later life Mary married his son), but the bond between them lasted until his death, with Mary relying heavily on the Catholic emperor for support and advice.

Thanks to her mother's efforts, Mary received a strict and thorough education. Her earliest teacher was Thomas Linacre, a Latin scholar who had been Prince Arthur's tutor, but he was soon replaced by the Spaniard Juan Luis Vives, who taught Mary from the ages of 8 to

Mary's Innocence

One of Mary's ladies in waiting reported that the queen was 'so bred as she knew no foul or unclean speeches', a fact illustrated by an incident that took place when Mary was in her 30s. The queen overheard her Lord Chamberlain calling one of her maids of honour a 'pretty whore'. Later the same day she exclaimed to the same maid, 'God-a mercy, my pretty whore!' When the maid begged Mary not to use such a shocking word, the queen was horrified. She had never heard the word before and had no idea of its meaning.

13. Vives gave Mary a firm grounding in the classics and scripture. He also held strong views on the upbringing of girls which he outlined for Mary's benefit in a treatise entitled *The Education of a Christian Woman*. The treatise makes fascinating reading for anyone attempting to understand Mary's personality. According to Vives, young girls should be trained for a life of humility, self-sacrifice and obedience. They should spend their time

in the company of virtuous women, and learn to weave and spin in order to induce in them a 'love of sober sadness'. Men should be avoided wherever possible, along with any romance or ribaldry, and teenage girls should strive to 'bridle the body and quench the fire of youth'. Viewed through modern eyes, it is clear that Mary's early education must have given her a sense of helplessness and dependence that would later blight her adult life.

Vives did not entirely succeed in breaking Mary's spirit. The young Princess Mary proved to be an able scholar, and a quiet, obedient child, but she also inherited a love of riding, hawking and hunting from her father. Like King Henry, she enjoyed music and dancing and became an accomplished performer on the lute and the virginals, even teaching some of her serving women how to play.

The young princess must have been all too aware that she was not the son that her father longed for, and, as the years went by, the problem of the lack of a male heir loomed ever larger over the royal household. One of the most important roles of the heir to the throne was to act as Prince of Wales, and when Mary was 9 years old, her father decided to take an unprecedented step. In the summer of 1525, Mary was sent to Ludlow Castle to preside over her own vice-regal court in the Welsh marches. For the next 18 months she assumed the role of Princess of Wales (although she was never formally invested with the title). While her council decided on matters of justice and taxation, the young princess practised for the role of sovereign, with a growing awareness that one day she might very well be queen.

Mary stayed in Ludlow until just after her 11th birthday, when threats of a Welsh rebellion made it expedient to disband the Royal Council. There were also major changes afoot in the English court – events that would turn Mary's childhood upside down. By the time that his daughter returned from Wales, King Henry had embarked on a determined campaign to annul his marriage to Catherine of Aragon and marry Anne Boleyn.

In the summer of 1527 Henry informed the queen of his intention to divorce her, setting in motion a process that was to drag on for the next five years. It was a wretched period for Mary, forced to witness her father's deliberate rejection of her mother and his open flirtation with the woman who was widely disparaged as 'the great whore'. The princess who had once been the darling of the court now rarely appeared in the king's presence, but instead she spent long hours with her grieving mother, watching the queen's desperate struggle to maintain her dignity. Between the ages of 11 and 17, Mary came face to face with some very harsh facts of life. She also contemplated an uncertain future as Henry's bastard daughter if he succeeded in getting his marriage annulled.

In July 1533, the 17-year-old Mary received a terrible message. She was informed that her parents' marriage had been pronounced invalid and that Henry and Anne were now man and wife. At the same time Mary was told that she could no longer communicate with her mother, either verbally by messenger or in writing. According to contemporary accounts, Mary remained composed as she received this news, even writing a letter to congratulate the king on his marriage. But inwardly she must have felt that her world had fallen apart.

Jane the Fool

The Lady Mary employed a company of jesters to provide amusement for herself and her household. These entertainers included an intriguing character known as Jane the Fool, and her companion, Lucretia the Tumbler. Jane had a wide repertoire of jokes, songs and tricks, and adopted a parody of court dress, combining silk and damask gowns with the hose and shoes of a clown. She was also as bald as an egg, and had her head shaved by a barber once a month to maintain the look.

For a few months after her father's wedding, Mary remained in her royal residence at Beaulieu north of Chelmsford, but this independence was not to last. Queen Anne was a famously vindictive woman who was determined to humiliate her stepdaughter. (She was even heard to boast that she would either poison Mary with 'too much dinner' or 'marry her to some varlet'.) In the event, the birth of her daughter provided Anne with the perfect method of punishing Mary. Within a month of the baby's birth, Mary was stripped of her title of princess, and ordered to move to Hatfield House, where she would serve as a maid of honour to the infant Princess Elizabeth.

Horror at Hatfield House

A few days before Christmas 1533, Mary was conveyed to Hatfield House. Now addressed simply as 'Lady Mary', she had been deprived of the company of most of her ladies, including the woman she looked upon as a substitute mother, Margaret Pole, Countess of Salisbury. Mary's arrival at Hatfield was later described by Eustache Chapuys, ambassador to the Holy Roman Emperor, who wrote that she was assigned 'the worst lodging in the house', where she retired to weep alone.

Chapuys feared the 'bad designs' of Mary's new caretakers – and he was not mistaken. A battle of wills soon developed as Mary adopted a position of determined dignity, while the members of Princess Elizabeth's household waged a deliberate campaign to humiliate her. On every occasion, Mary refused to answer to the title of Lady Mary or to address her half-sister as Princess. In return, she was punished, first by the confiscation of her jewels and clothes and then by deliberate abuse. Chief among the persecutors was her 'governess', Lady Shelton, the aunt of Anne Boleyn, who took to slapping and swearing at Mary whenever she claimed to be a true princess. When visitors arrived hoping to see the Lady Mary, her governess made sure that she was locked in her room and even nailed the windows shut. Anyone who treated Mary with kindness and respect was dismissed. Most distressing of all to Mary were her father's visits to see Elizabeth, which were preceded by orders that his older daughter should be locked out of sight in her room.

Two weeks before her 19th birthday Mary became seriously ill. By this time she had begun to suffer from a range of disorders, including stomach pains, headaches and depression, that were to dog her for the rest of her life, but this attack was especially frightening. As she lay in bed, wracked by pain and fever, there were even rumours that she was being poisoned. Recognizing the seriousness of the situation, Henry decided to send her away from Hatfield. Only when she was settled in the royal palace at Greenwich did Mary begin to recover, although her health was not improved by the constant presence of Lady Shelton dropping heavy hints that Mary would be better off dead.

Mary was still weak and depressed when she received some very distressing news. On 12 January 1536, Lady Shelton informed the Lady Mary 'most unceremoniously without the least preparation' that her mother was dead. It had been more than three years since Mary had last seen Catherine and she was not permitted to attend her mother's funeral. Meanwhile, there were reports that Henry and Anne were holding public rejoicings to celebrate Catherine's death. Mary must have felt that the future looked very dark, but in fact her fortunes were about to change. In the space of just four months, Anne Boleyn was executed and King Henry had taken Jane Seymour as his new wife.

All The King's Children

Jane Seymour's attitude to the Lady Mary was the complete opposite of Anne Boleyn's. With touching naivety, she pressed for a return of Henry's daughter to his side, convinced that such an example of family unity would inspire the nation. And Henry did not need much persuasion. Sometime in the summer of 1536, Mary was summoned for her first encounter with her father in five years, riding through the night to meet him in a house outside London.

It must have been an emotional meeting. In the difficult years since father and daughter had last seen one another, Mary had matured into a woman. In the place of his troubled teenage daughter, Henry was confronted with a strikingly intelligent-looking woman of 20, with a penetrating gaze, a determined mouth and a startlingly deep and powerful voice. From mid-afternoon until vespers, father and daughter remained together – in the words of one observer – 'conversing in private and with such love and affection, and such brilliant promises for the future that no father could have behaved better to his daughter.' Henry, it was reported, expressed deep regret at having been parted from Mary for so long, and conveyed a gift from Jane Seymour. She had sent a valuable diamond ring and the message that preparations were in place for Mary to be welcomed back to court.

Mary's return to court was delayed for several months, while her father completed his annual summer hunting tour. In the meantime, Mary divided her time between establishing her new household at Hunsdon in Hertfordshire, and regular visits to Hatfield House. Freed of the irksome presence of Lady Shelton, Mary began to enjoy the company of the Lady Elizabeth, then aged nearly 3, and Mary's letters to King Henry included fond reports about the remarkable gifts of the young Elizabeth.

Mary looked forward keenly to the end of her exile, but there was still a major obstacle in her way. King Henry insisted that before she returned to court, she should first sign a document acknowledging her mother's marriage to be incestuous and unlawful. Under tremendous pressure from her father she at last capitulated and signed the document, but she never forgave herself for betraying her mother's memory. When Mary joined King Henry and Queen Jane that Christmas, there was rejoicing among the common people, who viewed her as a wronged fairytale princess, but there was also sadness on her part. In the words of ambassador Chapuys there were still 'a few drachmas of gall and bitterness mixed with the sweet food of paternal kindness'.

The brief interlude of family unity created by Queen Jane was short-lived. October brought the birth of

Prince Edward, rapidly followed by the death of the queen, and Mary found herself taking on the role of chief mourner at Jane's funeral. As King Henry plunged into a demanding round of diplomatic duties, Mary established a routine of her own, walking for several miles in the mornings, reading from the classics and playing the virginals. Mary never neglected her devotions, reading from the Bible and attending Mass every day, but she also enjoyed secular pleasures such as riding, hunting, and playing card games and bowls.

Mary had a talent for creating close bonds with those around her, and the members of her court received many thoughtful gifts from their royal mistress. On her daily walks, she carried a purse full of pennies, ready to give to anyone in need, and she was especially generous to impoverished nuns, monks and priests. Ambassadors who visited Mary at this time were impressed by her fresh complexion and youthful looks, but above all they admired her 'very great goodness and discretion'. In short, she was a thoroughly eligible bride. And yet the Lady Mary remained unmarried. As an illegitimate princess her position was ambiguous. And following the birth of Prince Edward, it must also have become obvious to her that Henry was unwilling to marry her off, in case her husband should attempt to claim the throne from Henry's son and heir.

King Henry had no such scruples about his own marriage. In January 1540 he married Anne of Cleves, who was swiftly succeeded by Catherine Howard. Mary had little to do with Anne, although she was welcomed to her court, but relations with Catherine proved somewhat trickier. Mary was only five years older than Catherine and she had several reasons to dislike her. Not only was the girl related to the hated Anne Boleyn, but her flirtatious manners would have been especially repugnant to Henry's prudish daughter. Mary must have found a way to make her feelings known because Queen Catherine was soon complaining that Mary failed to treat her with proper respect, and the young queen even persuaded Henry to dismiss two of Mary's serving ladies. A hasty exchange of gifts between Mary and Catherine went some way to smoothing over the disagreement, but their quarrel was soon history. In February 1542 Catherine was dispatched to the Tower and King Henry was single again.

The period following Catherine's execution marked a low point for Henry. By now the king was obese, bad tempered and ill, and he turned increasingly to his older daughter for comfort and companionship. In the year following Catherine's execution, Henry invited Mary to oversee the Christmas celebrations 'in default of a queen', and over the next few months he lavished gifts on his daughter, visiting her in her chamber two or three times a day. Henry's marriage to Catherine Parr in 1543 must have come as a welcome relief for Mary, who recognized in her father's sixth wife a woman of intelligence, piety and good sense who would share the burden of caring for the ailing king.

In the last four years of Henry's life, Mary was often at court, in the company of the king and queen and the

Lady Elizabeth and Prince Edward. Queen Catherine became a close companion for Mary, and she also enjoyed the company of Elizabeth and Edward (who were 9 and 5 years old at the time of their father's last marriage). In those few precious years, Mary got to know her siblings in a way she had never done before. However, as Henry's death approached, his children must have recognized that their new-found closeness would soon be sorely tested. Once the young King Edward came to the throne, he might face a rebellion springing from the rival claims of Mary or Elizabeth. And the Lady Mary posed a particular threat to her young brother. As a devoted follower of the old Catholic faith, she could be a rallying point for discontented Catholics. After Henry's death, it was horribly clear that Edward's 'most loved sister', as he once called her, would be a major threat to his security as king.

Mary and Edward: Keeping the Faith

King Henry died a month before Mary's 31st birthday.

Edward was crowned king and Mary took the precaution of withdrawing to East Anglia, where she moved between her royal residences. Wherever Mary stayed, her household always included a priest to hold regular services, and bells were rung to summon the local people to Mass, creating a small Roman Catholic community in her vicinity.

As England under Edward moved inexorably towards Protestantism, Mary intensified her devotions, hearing up to four Masses a day. She also became increasingly dependent on visits from the ambassadors of the Holy Roman Emperor. Mary had always seen Emperor Charles V as a father-figure and protector. Now, with Charles' encouragement, she began to believe that her personal destiny was to keep the Catholic faith alive in England.

Ever since the start of Edward's reign, Mary had been on the receiving end of ominous messages from the Royal Council, instructing her to desist from holding Mass. However, in 1549 her adherence to the old faith became a punishable offence. Edward's new Act of

Uniformity outlawed the Mass, replacing it with services from the *Book of Common Prayer*. On the day that Mary learned of the Act, she ordered her chaplains to celebrate an especially ceremonial Mass in her chapel at Kenninghall in Norfolk. She also wrote a letter to Charles V announcing, 'In life or death, I will not forsake the Catholic religion … even if compelled thereto by threats or violence.'

Such dangerous defiance could not go unpunished for long. A series of demands that Mary should obey the law were followed by attempts to intimidate her personal chaplain and servants. But all these threats simply strengthened Mary's resolve. Eventually, the Lord Protector succumbed to some subtle pressure from the Holy Roman Emperor, and the Lady Mary's household was granted the right to attend the Mass 'privately in her own apartment'.

In 1549 John Dudley wrested control over the king from Edward Seymour, and the danger to Mary increased. Dudley was implacably opposed to Mary, claiming that she was 'the conduit by which the rats of Rome might creep into the stronghold'. He accused her of being at the heart of a series of uprisings against the government. In fact, Mary was innocent of all conspiracies, but she now entered into a plot of her own, as she prepared to escape to the continent and the protection of Emperor Charles V. In the event, the plans came to nothing, but not before she had spent an agonizing few days on the Kent coast, wracked with indecision over whether she should join the imperial ships waiting for her in the Channel.

Where his Royal Council had failed to persuade the Lady Mary, the young King Edward believed that he could succeed, and at the age of 13 he began to issue a series of letters and writs addressed to his sister. Such stern reproaches from her beloved brother caused Mary great personal suffering, but they failed to shake her resolve. Even when Edward sent his officers to Mary's home, intent on arresting all those involved in Catholic practices, Mary still defied him by hiding one of her priests. It seemed the battle of wills would continue indefinitely – until Edward's illness changed everything.

By February 1553, rumours about the king's ill health were rife, and Mary was determined to find out the truth for herself. With little regard for her personal safety, she rode to London, where she waited for three days before being admitted to see the king. When at last she saw her brother, it was obvious that he was dying, and she talked with him gently, avoiding any discussion of religion. Mary was greatly saddened by Edward's sufferings, but she was also concerned for her own safety. As the next in line to the throne, she stood directly in the way of Dudley's ambitions – and it was clear that he would not abandon power without a struggle.

Claiming the Crown

Mary was staying in Hertfordshire when she received a message summoning her to the bedside of her dying brother. Fearing a trap, she proceeded cautiously, but before she got to Greenwich, she was warned to stay away. So she headed east for Norfolk instead. By the time she arrived at Kenninghall, on 9 July, events had moved very fast. Edward had been dead for three days, and Dudley's son was heading east to capture her. Mary responded decisively, pronouncing herself rightful Queen of England in front of her assembled household and sending a message to Dudley ordering him to proclaim her as sovereign. Meanwhile other messengers were dispatched across East Anglia 'to draw the gentlemen of the surrounding kingdom to do fealty to their sovereign'.

Mary's message reached the Tower of London just as Dudley was hosting a banquet for Queen Jane. When it was read aloud, it caused great consternation among the assembled councillors. Encouraged by Dudley, they had somehow believed that Mary would be easily captured and controlled, but now she had proved them wrong. Nevertheless, few believed that Mary could overcome Dudley and be crowned queen. Even the Emperor

Charles feared that such open defiance would have tragic consequences, and urged his ambassadors to persuade Mary to submit to Queen Jane.

But Mary had set an unstoppable process in motion. Within hours of her proclamation, gentlemen and peasants were flocking to her support, and by 12 July she had moved to Framlingham Castle close to the Suffolk coast from where she was rallying her forces. When reports arrived that Dudley was leading an army against her from London, Mary was ready to resist. Her supporters numbered around 15,000 and were growing steadily, as one by one the towns of the south-east began to proclaim Mary as their queen.

By 16 July, Mary's band of supporters had grown to 30,000. There was also heartening news from the fleet of ships that Dudley had stationed off the coast. Rather than following Dudley's orders, the captain of the fleet had decided to switch sides and serve Mary instead. Finally, on 18 July, Dudley was forced to admit defeat. The following day Mary was proclaimed queen in London amid wild celebrations, bonfires and ringing of bells.

With great determination and unshakeable belief in her cause, Mary had achieved a virtual miracle, and on 3 August 1553, she rode in triumph into London.

Mary the Queen

The English welcomed Mary as the rightful heir to the throne who would restore their much-damaged kingdom. Throughout Edward's reign they had witnessed the plots of ambitious men scheming behind the scenes, and now at last they had an adult monarch on the throne. Mary played up to the crowds by dressing in sumptuous gowns covered in flashing jewels, and looking every inch the dignified queen as she rode through the streets of London. After the turmoil of the past few years, the people were prepared to take Queen Mary to their hearts, but no one had any idea what kind of ruler she would turn out to be.

In fact, the English people had almost no experience

of being ruled by a queen. The only woman to have ruled England was Queen Matilda, back in the 12th century, and people looked back in horror to her chaotic reign as a time when 'god and his saints slept'. In Tudor society, women were not perceived as figures of authority and a single woman like Mary, with no real experience of the world of men, was at a massive disadvantage at court. Nevertheless, the new queen possessed some sterling qualities. She was virtuous, kind, truthful, affectionate and conscientious. However, she was also convinced that God was on her side, and could be dangerously blinkered and obstinate once she had embarked on a course of action.

In the early months of her reign, it was Mary's gentle side that was most apparent. To the dismay of her advisers, she refused to punish most of those involved in the proclamation of Lady Jane Grey as queen. While Dudley was executed, his followers merely received a mild rebuke from their queen. Mary also insisted that Jane was innocent, making it clear that she should remain in the Tower for a short period only, until the time was right to release her. Mary was also keen to reassure her people that they would not be persecuted for pursuing their Protestant religion (a position she was later to abandon). As she explained to her councillors, it was not her intention 'to compel or constrain other men's consciences', and in her first official announcement as queen she made it plain that she meant to leave her subjects free to worship as they chose until Parliament was ready to bring about orderly change. Meanwhile, the royal court led the way in traditional observance, with six or seven Masses a day being held in Queen Mary's chapel. At the same time, altars were restored and crucifixes replaced, as priests began to celebrate Roman Catholic services in their traditional form.

All these changes did not go unopposed, and passionate demonstrations were staged all over the land. In London, a dagger was hurled at Mary's chaplain, Gilbert Bourne, after he had preached a sermon denouncing Nicholas Ridley, the former Bishop of

London. Bourne was unharmed, but passions had been inflamed and were hard to subdue.

Religion also divided Mary's council, who quarrelled amongst each other constantly, rendering decision-making almost impossible. In the first weeks of her reign, Mary had appointed Stephen Gardiner as Lord Chancellor and head of the council. Gardiner had been Bishop of Winchester under King Henry, and had spent most of Edward's reign under lock and key in the Tower before he was released by Mary. A consummate politician, he asserted his will with ruthless efficiency, but made many enemies in the council and the country as a consequence.

One of the most pressing issues facing Mary was the threat from France. King Henry II had taken advantage of England's weakness during the final months of King Edward's reign, and the French were preparing to take back the English-held territories of Calais and Guisnes. As a gesture of her serious intent, Mary organized a muster of fighting men to reinforce the defence of these strategic lands. Her preventive measure worked – at least in the short term – and Henry was dissuaded from carrying out his attack.

Mary soon discovered that her country faced serious financial difficulties. By the end of July 1554, she had run out of funds to cover her current expenses. Dudley had left enormous debts and creditors were pressing on all sides. Somewhat unrealistically, Mary saw it a point of honour that all royal debts should be paid, and announced in September that she would pay off every obligation left from the two preceding reigns – no matter how long it took. She also took significant steps to solve the long-term crisis in the English currency. During the reigns of Henry VIII and Edward VI, there had been frequent 'debasements' of English coins, as their gold and silver content was replaced with cheaper metals such as copper. This short-term expedient had the result of liberating more wealth, but led to a lack of confidence amongst foreign merchants. Under Queen Mary, new coins were issued containing higher proportions of gold and silver and the queen announced there would be no more debasements of the English coinage. Thanks to these efforts, English money gradually began to hold its value in European markets. Mary had made a strong and determined start as a monarch, but there were major challenges ahead.

Marriage and Rebellion

Right from the start of Mary's reign one burning question was on everyone's lips. Did the queen plan to take a husband, and – if so – who? Several suitable candidates were suggested, including Edward Courtenay, a young nobleman with royal connections, who would provide a suitable but harmless husband to the queen. However, Mary had just one man in mind. She was fervently hoping for a match with Prince Philip of Spain, the son of her long-term protector, the Holy Roman Emperor. At 27 years of age, Philip was eleven years younger than Mary, and, by all accounts, a dignified, serious, but rather dull young man. Philip's pompous manner made him deeply unpopular with the Spanish people, but this was not what most worried Mary's advisers. As heir to the Hapsburg Empire, Philip was due to inherit from his ailing father total control of Spain and the Netherlands, as well as substantial parts of the New World. If Mary married Philip, England risked simply becoming an insignificant part of his vast Hapsburg dominions. Even more alarmingly, England would be ruled by a Catholic monarch with very close links to the pope – an unthinkable prospect for English Protestants.

Against this background of fervent opposition, Mary obstinately pursued her dream. On 8 November 1554, she announced her intention of marrying Philip. The public outcry against 'Jack Spaniard' was immediate, with some leading Protestants announcing that they would rather die than let the Spaniards rule their country. Parliament led a delegation to the queen, begging her to marry an Englishman. But Mary was adamant and in January a marriage treaty was concluded with Emperor

Charles V. The announcement of the treaty caused widespread dismay, and four noblemen resolved to take drastic action. Sir Thomas Wyatt from Kent, Sir James Crofts from Herefordshire, Sir Peter Carew from Devon and Henry Grey from Leicestershire (the father of Lady Jane Grey) each prepared to raise a rebellion in his own area, with the aim of converging on London. The conspirators' ultimate aim was to replace Mary with her half-sister Elizabeth who would marry Edward Courtenay. Meanwhile a fleet of French ships would prevent Philip of Spain from reaching England by sea.

All was progressing well, until Simon Renard, the Emperor's ambassador in England, began to suspect some kind of plot. Renard reported his suspicions to Stephen Gardiner, who questioned Courtenay until he revealed the plans. Of the four rebel leaders, three eventually abandoned their attempts, but Wyatt remained determined to lead an uprising against the queen. On 26 January 1554 Wyatt and a band of supporters occupied the Kentish town of Rochester.

From there he issued a proclamation to the people of Kent, who flocked to join him. At first, Mary's supporters, led by Lord Abergavenny and Sir Robert Southwell, managed to suppress the uprising, but gradually they were deserted by their men, who either left the army or joined Wyatt's rebels. By the end of January, Wyatt had 3,000 men under his command. Mary sent the aged Duke of Norfolk to lead an attack on the rebels, but this campaign proved to be a disaster as Norfolk's troops promptly swapped sides, raising the numbers of Wyatt's men to 4,000, while the Duke fled back to London.

The woeful sight of Norfolk struggling back to London must have struck horror into Mary's heart, but when she turned to her council for help she found them quarrelsome and unsupportive. While some of her councillors remained worryingly silent, others urged the queen to flee. Mary, however, remained resolute in the face of danger. On 1 February she delivered a rousing speech at the Guildhall, reminding her subjects of their duty of allegiance and obedience to their sovereign, and assuring them that she was only contemplating marriage as a way 'to leave some fruit of my body behind me to be your governor'. It was a rousing speech and thousands rallied to her support. But Mary was not yet out of danger.

On the morning of Saturday 3 February, Wyatt's army arrived in Southwark, where they met no serious resistance. But when they prepared to cross the River Thames, they found that Mary's supporters had occupied London Bridge, preventing the rebels from crossing it and so entering the city. Meanwhile, Sir John Bridges was threatening to use the guns at the Tower to fire on Southwark. Faced with the danger of bombardment, Wyatt made the decision to march to Kingston, where the rebels had to rebuild a bridge before they could eventually cross the river. Once north of the Thames, Wyatt managed to lead his men as far as Ludgate, before they were finally forced to turn back, only to discover that all their escape routes were blocked. To prevent more bloodshed, Wyatt surrendered and by nightfall his rebel army had dispersed. Wyatt was tried and executed, along with around ninety fellow conspirators, and their rotting bodies were left hanging from the gallows as a gruesome example to any future rebels. Others were more fortunate. Bound with cords and wearing nooses around their necks, they walked in double file to the tiltyard at Westminster where they knelt in the mud before Mary. There she pardoned them before their ropes were cut and the nooses were thrown off in a public ceremony of repentance and absolution. Lady Jane Grey was also caught up in the wave of retribution, as Mary decided reluctantly that she and her husband should be put to death. Not only had Jane's father played a prominent part in the plot, but Jane, if left alive, might prove a dangerous rallying point for any future rebellions.

If Lady Jane Grey posed a threat to Mary's security, the Lady Elizabeth was many times more dangerous. When she had first arrived in London as queen, Mary had ridden into the city with Elizabeth at her side. But as Mary's popularity declined, she had been persuaded by her advisers to regard her half-sister as a threat. Not only was Elizabeth younger and more beautiful than her older sister, she was also a Protestant and a natural figurehead around which any rebellion against Mary's reforms might coalesce. This argument became horribly clear when it emerged that some of the rebels in Wyatt's uprising had approached the Lady Elizabeth for her support.

Once the rebellion had been quelled, Elizabeth was summoned before the council. There, she cleverly managed to distance herself from any involvement with Wyatt's plot. It appeared that Elizabeth was innocent, but while she was at liberty she endangered Mary's security. For the next three months Elizabeth was imprisoned in the Tower, before being sent to Woodstock Palace near Oxford, where she was to spend the following year under house arrest.

Wyatt's uprising failed to prevent Queen Mary's marriage. In late July 1554 Prince Philip arrived in England to meet his prospective bride. At their first meeting, Philip behaved with perfect gallantry, although he later described Queen Mary as 'rather older than we had been told'. Others in his party were less discreet, and one complained that 'the queen is not at all beautiful ... small and rather flabby than fat, she is of white complexion and fair, and has no eyebrows.'

Two days after their first meeting, Philip and Mary were married in Winchester Cathedral, with a solemn nuptial Mass to mark the event. The ceremony was followed by a splendid banquet for the Spanish and English courtiers but their many differences in language and culture meant that the event was not a great success. Nor did the royal couple appear to have much to say to one another. The morning after his wedding night, Philip rose at seven and worked at his desk until eleven when he went to Mass and then dined alone.

Just three months after her marriage to Philip, Mary let it be known that she was pregnant. The good news caused some softening of the public's attitude to Philip, although it also raised the question of his official status. Philip was now pressing hard to be crowned King of

England, but Mary still resisted, recognizing that this would be a step too far for her subjects. By this time, Philip was also desperate to leave for Flanders, where the French were threatening his territories. But he resolved to stay in England until the birth of his child. In Easter Week 1555, the queen travelled to Hampton Court for her confinement and everybody waited in trepidation, anticipating a difficult birth. By the end of April, however, there was still no news and some worrying rumours had begun to circulate. It had been observed that the queen's belly was much less swollen than before. Perhaps she had deceived herself and had never been pregnant after all?

As the weeks dragged by and the queen still failed to give birth, the embarrassing truth became apparent. Somehow Mary and her doctors had been mistaken about her pregnancy. It was indisputable that she had displayed some symptoms consistent with being pregnant, but these could have been due to some other physical or psychological cause. By the time nine months had passed, most of Mary's symptoms had disappeared, and in August she left Hampton Court with as little public ceremony as possible, determined to concentrate on the urgent task of ruling the country.

Why Did Mary Believe She Was Pregnant?

According to contemporary reports, Mary displayed a range of symptoms that indicated she was pregnant. These signs included the ceasing of her periods, a swollen stomach and some discharge of milk from her breasts. Some of these symptoms can be attributed to amenorrhoea, a condition that Mary had suffered from since she was a teenager, which causes painful and irregular periods and swelling of the abdomen and the breasts. Some historians have suggested that Mary experienced a 'phantom pregnancy' with a range of psychosomatic symptoms induced by the hysterical belief that she was expecting a child. Others have considered the possibility that she had a disorder of the pituitary gland or a cancerous tumour in her womb.

Bloody Mary

When Mary was just one month into her imagined pregnancy, Cardinal Reginald Pole arrived from Rome, signalling that the queen's programme of Catholic reform had begun in earnest. On 25 November 1554, Parliament repealed Henry's Act of Supremacy and five days later Cardinal Pole welcomed the English people back into the fold of the Catholic Church. On 18 December Parliament revived the medieval heresy laws. These laws granted bishops the right to hand over anyone suspected of heresy to the secular authorities for burning at the stake.

The blame for the orgy of burnings that followed must be laid firmly at Mary's feet. Most of her advisers, including her husband, urged her to proceed with caution. But Mary had a simple, unwavering belief that heretics were destined for an eternity of hellfire. Surely, she reasoned, it was better for a few to burn here on Earth as an example to the many. Convinced of these beliefs, Mary urged the authorities to be diligent in seeking out heresy and punishing it with death.

The first executions took place in February 1555, when a commission headed by Bishop Gardiner condemned five people to death for heresy. Among the first to be burned was John Hooper, Bishop of Gloucester, who suffered an agonizing death. The gunpowder bag hung around his neck, intended to speed his death when it exploded, failed to ignite and he burned for three quarters of an hour, begging the crowd to fan the flames and end his agony. The bravery with which the martyrs endured their punishment sparked off a passionate public outcry, hardening people's resolve to stay true to their Protestant faith, but the burnings continued relentlessly. Over the next three years, 240 men and sixty women died at the stake.

Some of the Protestants condemned to be burned alive were very high-profile figures, such as the former Archbishop Thomas Cranmer and the bishops Hugh Latimer and Nicholas Ridley. But most of those who died were poor and ignorant labourers and traders. These unfortunate victims were often condemned to death by Catholic fanatics simply because they could not recite the Lord's Prayer or explain exactly what the Sacraments were. There were even martyrs who were blind or disabled, and one woman was pregnant. As she was suffering in her death agony, her baby was born – only for it to be cast back into the flames by the executioner.

While Protestant martyrs burned in English market places, other changes were taking place in the rites of religious observance. Catholic services and feast days were reinstated, parish priests were banned from marrying and Cranmer's *Book of Common Prayer* was systematically repressed. These unwelcome changes, coupled with Mary's persecution of heretics, led to a steady exodus of Protestants from England. During Mary's reign, hundreds of men and women slipped across the channel, heading for sanctuary in Switzerland and Germany. Among the exiles were many ordinary folk – farmers, blacksmiths, masons and labourers – as well as preachers and scholars determined to make their protest heard. Two early exiles were the fiery Scots preacher, John Knox, an outspoken critic of the queen, and the historian, John Foxe, who was later to compile Foxe's *Book of Martyrs*, detailing the horrors of Mary's reign. German printing presses churned out passionate anti-Marian propaganda, and pamphlets denouncing Mary as a Jezebel and a papist whore were smuggled into England. Meanwhile ballads circulated that glorified the martyrs who had died for their faith, and reviled the clergy who had sent them to their deaths. In this atmosphere of mounting resentment, the air was thick with rumours of plots to overthrow the queen. In the closing days of 1555 Mary wrote to Philip that 'she was encompassed with enemies and could not move without endangering her crown'.

Mary and France

By the time she reached her 40s, Mary was a deeply disappointed woman. Her campaign to root out heresy had not just made her universally hated, but had managed to stiffen the resolve of the Protestants, while her efforts to restore the Catholic faith had failed to bear fruit. By 1557, abbeys, convents and shrines were still in ruins, most churches lacked candlesticks, service books and vestments, and many parish priests were married and knew no Latin. After three years on the throne, Mary had forfeited the love and support of her subjects, and she watched with mounting anxiety as the Lady Elizabeth took her place in the hearts of the English people. Queen Mary also had to deal with a private grief. Following the fiasco of her false pregnancy, Prince Philip had left for the Netherlands, and had stayed away ever since. Mary's frequent letters to her husband went unanswered, and there were rumours that Philip was enjoying a life of tournaments and womanizing.

Faced with these disappointments, the queen plunged herself into a routine of devotions and acts of charity. She became well known for her visits to the poor, when she dressed very simply and appeared filled with concern. Following these visits, needy families were given money and clothes, and sons were found apprenticeships, while the queen took it upon herself to pursue cases of injustice. All these self-imposed duties, coupled with a conscientious approach to her work with the Royal Council, had a damaging effect on her health, and she was often laid low with fevers and depression.

In the autumn of 1556, Mary learnt that her husband was planning to visit England. She was delighted at the prospect, although she must have realized that his motives were purely political. Philip had now inherited the title of King of Spain and was planning a war against northern France, for which he needed England's support.

King Philip finally arrived in March of 1557 and the queen ordered that all the bells in London should ring to welcome him home. The reunion of Philip and Mary was fraught with difficulties. Both of them had aged noticeably and Philip's entourage included his latest mistress. Despite these evident tensions, Mary was anxious to please her husband, and succumbed to his pressure over the war with France. Even though her council was strongly opposed to a war that would disrupt trade and bankrupt the crown, Mary overruled her advisers and promised English support, stirring up a storm of anti-Spanish feeling in the country.

On 6 July, Mary bade a fond farewell to her husband as he set out for France. With the support of the English forces that he had enlisted, Philip's French campaign proved to be a success. In August, he captured the town of St Quentin, claiming many distinguished French nobles as prisoners. This victory was followed by some smaller gains, and by a satisfactory diplomatic treaty. By October, Philip had ordered most of his troops to disband, but King Henry II was not yet finished with the English. He had recognized the perfect time to launch an attack on the port of Calais, the last major English possession on the continent.

In December, the French prepared to attack Calais.

The town was poorly guarded and the freezing weather favoured the French, who could approach over the frozen waters of the surrounding marshes. Mary responded as swiftly as possible, giving orders for ships to set sail from Dover, but by then the French had already launched an attack by sea. On 13 January 1558 French cannon fire breached the city walls and triumphant French troops took possession of the town. The fall of Calais was followed by the capture of Guîsnes and Ham, England's other holdings in France. The last English foothold in foreign territory had been lost.

The End of a Reign

For Mary, the fall of Calais was a devastating blow, although its force was somewhat softened by more hopeful news. Once again, the queen believed that she was pregnant. This time she delayed informing Philip until she was certain, but by December she wrote that there were 'very sure signs' that she would deliver a child in March. Mindful of 'the great danger' of childbirth, Mary drew up a will, leaving the crown to her unborn child and nominating Philip as regent during the child's minority.

By February 1558, Mary's councillors were pressing her to attend to the urgent problem of her country's finances. Throughout Mary's reign, England had struggled with a depressed economy and serious debts, and now these problems were exacerbated by the costs of the French war. Mary's council held daily meetings to try to find a way to make ends meet, but their queen was strangely disengaged, and there was a sense that she was slipping away from the world. To make matters worse, the queen's closest adviser, Cardinal Pole, was also fading fast, and becoming increasingly vague and incoherent.

By May no baby had been born, and it was clear that Mary's distended belly was the outward sign of a fatal 'dropsy', an accumulation of liquid under the skin and inside the body, generally leading to kidney failure. As her illness advanced, the queen became feverish and by August her doctors were predicting that she did not have long to live. Mary finally died on the morning of 17 November 1558, aged 42. Sometime before her death, she had made the doleful prediction that those who opened her body after her death would find the words 'Philip' and 'Calais' inscribed on her heart.

Chapter 7
THE MAKING OF A GREAT QUEEN – YOUNG ELIZABETH

Princess Elizabeth was born on 7 September 1533 in the royal palace at Greenwich, the daughter of Henry VIII and Anne Boleyn. Mother and baby were well, but the royal birth was not a cause for great rejoicing. Henry knew that Anne was deeply unpopular among his subjects, but he had gambled that she would give him a longed-for son and heir. Now he hastily cancelled the tournament planned to welcome a baby prince, and came to terms with the fact that he had a second daughter.

It was not an auspicious start for the child who would later become one of England's greatest monarchs. But, as she grew older, Elizabeth was to amaze all who knew her. By the time she ascended the throne, at the age of 25, she had already shown that she was a young woman of unusual intelligence and strength of character. By the end of her 44-year reign, England's 'Virgin Queen' had thoroughly disproved her father's belief that only a man was fit to rule.

The Infant Princess

After the celebrations for Elizabeth's christening, life quickly returned to normal at court and the infant princess was taken away to the country to be cared for quietly. By December a new household had been established for Elizabeth at Hatfield House in Hertfordshire, some 16 miles north of the capital. There, the young princess was placed in the care of two gentlewomen: Lady Margaret Bryan, who had also taken charge of the Princess Mary, and Lady Anne Shelton, aunt to Anne Boleyn. Altogether, Elizabeth's household totalled around twenty, including wet nurses, rockers and laundresses, a treasurer and several grooms. Also installed at Hatfield House was an extremely reluctant guest: Elizabeth's half-sister, the 17-year-old Princess Mary.

Whenever their royal schedule permitted a visit to Hatfield, Henry and Anne rode out to see their daughter. But there was little time for mother and child to get to know one another. When Elizabeth was less than 3 years old, Anne was executed for treason, and her daughter was declared illegitimate. The young Elizabeth must have missed her glamorous mother's visits, and she would certainly have noticed that those around her had suddenly ceased to address her as 'princess'. The gifts of fine clothes came to an end too. Three months after Anne's death, Margaret Bryan was writing plaintively to Thomas Cromwell begging him to supply raiment for the Lady Elizabeth, as she had 'neither gown, nor kirtle, nor petticoat'.

Growing Up

Less than a fortnight after Anne Boleyn's death, King Henry married Jane Seymour, one of the queen's ladies in waiting. Henry's gentle new wife encouraged him to see his daughters regularly, but the real change in Elizabeth's life came with the birth of Prince Edward, when she had just turned four. In a deliberate display of family unity, both Henry's daughters played a significant role in Edward's christening, with Mary acting as godmother to the infant prince and Elizabeth carrying the precious chrisom cloth to be wrapped around Prince Edward's head. Watching the ceremony from her uncle Edward Seymour's arms, Elizabeth cannot have failed to realize that her baby brother was now the most important child in the kingdom. She must also have been shocked by the sudden death of her stepmother nine days later.

Sometime in the summer of 1537, Catherine Champernowne was appointed as governess to the 4-year-old Lady Elizabeth. Better known by her married name, Catherine (or Kat) Ashley was to remain Elizabeth's closest companion for the next thirty years. As the daughter of a scholar and antiquarian, Kat belonged to a circle of educated gentry who enjoyed debating the latest humanist ideas, and she made it her mission to instruct Elizabeth in reading, writing and morals. Many years later, Elizabeth paid tribute to Kat's 'great labour and pain in bringing me up in learning and honesty'. Perhaps even most importantly, Kat Ashley seems to have provided the motherless Elizabeth with some much-needed emotional security. Catherine had a remarkably able pupil in the young Elizabeth. An astonished visitor reported that the 5-year-old conducted herself 'with as great gravity as if she had been forty years old' and continued enthusiastically 'If she were no more educated than she appears [now] she will be an honour to all womanhood'. The scholar Roger Ascham (who would later become one of Elizabeth's tutors) was also greatly impressed with her progress, although he urged Kat not to push her young pupil too hard. Elizabeth may have been unstoppable in her pursuit of learning, but she was far from being simply a bookworm. From an early age, she enjoyed riding, hunting and hawking and had a passion for music and dancing. She could play the lute and the virginals as well as singing and writing music. She also worked hard at her sewing and embroidery, and at the age of 5 she presented her baby brother with a shirt she had made herself.

Until she was 9 years old, Elizabeth continued to live quietly in the country, spending most of her time at Hatfield House. She saw little of her father, and her half-brother Edward had his own household, although the two royal children were often together. With just four years separating them, Elizabeth and Edward were natural companions; both were precociously fond of study, and both had lost their mothers at an early age. During these years, Elizabeth encountered two more stepmothers – Anne of Cleves and Catherine Howard. Neither wife had much to do with the young Elizabeth, although Catherine was related to her on her mother's side, but Catherine's dramatic execution, when Elizabeth was just 8 years old, must have had an impact on her, forcing her to remember her own mother's death.

In her father's sixth wife, Elizabeth finally found a stepmother she could admire and trust. Catherine Parr made all Henry's children welcome at court. She also helped to establish a new educational routine for Elizabeth and Edward. By the time she was 10 years old, Elizabeth was benefitting from the teaching of some outstanding scholars. William Grindal, a brilliant Cambridge man, was her chief tutor until she was 15, and when he died from the plague, his place was

The Sporting Life

Elizabeth participated in a range of sports. She went out hunting and hawking whenever she could, practised archery, and enjoyed long walks and rides several times a week. As part of her daily exercise routine, she liked to dance the galliard, an energetic dance with rapid hopping steps and spectacular leaps. Elizabeth also appreciated a range of spectator sports, including jousting, bearbaiting and cockfighting. Other popular Tudor sports were real tennis, fencing and bowls. Poorer people held wrestling and hammer-throwing contests and sometimes whole villages would take part in a riotous game of football and hurling (a type of field hockey).

taken by the multi-talented humanist Roger Ascham.

As she approached her teens, Elizabeth spent more time at court. She was encouraged by her stepmother to take part in lively debates on religion, and saw Catherine acting as regent while her father was away at war – a valuable example of a woman operating in the world of men. In this period, Elizabeth also observed the dramatic decline of her father into a sick, short-tempered and bloated old man. Yet, despite his many flaws, Henry remained an inspiration to his younger daughter. As queen, Elizabeth would often appeal to the public memory of Good King Hal, and she made a deliberate attempt to follow her father's example as an all-powerful, larger-than-life monarch.

King Henry's death had long been expected, but it still came as a blow to his 13-year-old daughter. Elizabeth was in the company of her brother when she learned the news that their father was dead and that Edward was the new king. Elizabeth prepared to face an uncertain future. As the illegitimate sister of the new king, she knew her position was far from secure. So she must have been grateful when her stepmother Catherine invited her to join her household.

Teenage Troubles

In the spring of 1547, Elizabeth moved into the Chelsea home of the dowager queen, Catherine Parr. There she quickly adapted to her new routine, continuing her studies with the 9-year-old Lady Jane Grey as her companion. However, her stepmother's home was to be the scene of some of the most disturbing incidents in Elizabeth's life.

Catherine had long been fond of Thomas Seymour, uncle to King Edward, but she had given him up to marry King Henry. Now that Henry was dead, however, Seymour once again appeared in Catherine's life. Tall, virile and handsome, with a bushy red beard, he was ruthlessly ambitious and had an eye for the ladies. Seymour's feelings for the dowager queen are not entirely clear, but they were probably fuelled by her wealth and status. By early summer, the couple had married and Thomas was living in Catherine's house with Elizabeth as his ward.

Seymour clearly revelled in the chance to get to know Elizabeth, and he was soon taking liberties with the growing girl, visiting her in her bedchamber while she was still in her nightdress, engaging in boisterous romps, and even smacking her playfully on the buttocks. Elizabeth for her part was partly aroused and partly terrified, cowering under her bedclothes in the mornings, afraid that Seymour would suddenly arrive unannounced. In this disturbing situation, Elizabeth's former mentors let her down badly. Kat Ashley failed to recognize just how damaging Seymour's advances were, both to Elizabeth's reputation and to her emotional stability, while her stepmother Catherine was so besotted by her new husband that she sometimes even joined in the tickling games. On one occasion, it was later reported, Catherine went so far as to hold her stepdaughter still while her husband cut Elizabeth's dress to shreds.

Eventually, however, something snapped in Catherine's brain. When she was five months pregnant she came across Seymour and Elizabeth locked in an embrace and recognized the threat to her marriage. Elizabeth was banished to the country, where she stayed in the home of Sir Anthony Denny, brother-in-law to Kat Ashley. Catherine must have felt hurt and angered by her husband's behaviour, but her bond with her stepdaughter was unbreakable, and Elizabeth was soon conveying her best wishes to Catherine for a safe delivery. Unfortunately, however, Catherine died in childbirth in September. Seymour claimed to be heartbroken at the death of his wife, but he was soon pursuing Elizabeth again, this time with marriage in mind – and Elizabeth was dangerously flattered.

Fortunately for Elizabeth, Seymour's scheming eventually caught up with him, and in early 1549 he was arrested, charged with attempting to kidnap the king and sent to the Tower. Following Seymour's imprisonment, the details of his flirtation with Elizabeth leaked out and the matter was pursued relentlessly by King Edward's officers. Some key members of Elizabeth's household were detained in the Tower until they had revealed all the details of the sordid, but essentially harmless, business. Even Elizabeth was not exempted from cross-examination. However, she countered all questions with great maturity, claiming that she was 'marvellous abashed' by the accusations. She later defended her honour in an outraged letter to the Lord Protector. In particular she was determined to deny the 'shameful slanders' about her morality, such as the rumour that she was 'with child' by Seymour.

Eventually it was decided that the matter should not be pursued any further and Seymour was executed for treason against the king. At the age of just 15, Elizabeth had learned some important lessons. She had discovered that she was attractive to men and she had enjoyed the sense of power that this gave her. But she had also been forced to recognize that sexual involvement was fraught with danger. As an adult woman, Elizabeth would use her feminine charms for her own ends. She would also endeavour – with varying degrees of success – to be ruled by her head, rather than her heart.

Elizabeth In Danger

Following the drama of the Seymour scandal, Elizabeth kept a low profile, living quietly in the country and concentrating on her studies. The scholar Roger Ascham spent the next two years coaching Elizabeth in classical studies, theology, French and Italian. Ascham delighted in the fact that his royal pupil could discourse intelligently on any subject, claiming that Elizabeth was 'the brightest star' of all the learned ladies in England, and asserting that her mind was free of the usual 'womanly weakness', being instead 'endued with a masculine power of application'.

Life at the royal court had little impact on Elizabeth in these years. Perhaps because her visits to the royal court were infrequent, the intimacy she had once shared with Edward had disappeared, and their

Humanism

Humanism was an intellectual movement that flourished in Europe during the Renaissance period. Drawing their inspiration from classical texts, the humanists rejected the narrow clerical approach of the medieval scholars, adopting a more 'human-centred' view of the world. Through the study of 'the humanities' (grammar, rhetoric, history, poetry and moral philosophy), humanists aimed to nurture men and women who could engage in civic life and persuade others to adopt virtuous and prudent actions. The movement began in Italy in the 14th century, and spread to northern Europe in the 1450s. The leading northern humanist was Desiderius Erasmus, who had a profound influence on English humanists such as Sir Thomas More and Elizabeth's tutor, Roger Ascham.

surviving letters to each other are stiff and formal. Even when she heard the news that her brother was dying, Elizabeth put caution first. Instead of rushing to be at Edward's side, she sent a message that she was ill and unable to travel. Then she waited to see how events would turn out in the wake of the king's death.

Elizabeth did well to keep away from court. Over the next few weeks, she watched from a safe distance as first Lady Jane Grey, and then her sister Mary, was hailed as queen. Only when it was clear that the crown was securely in Mary's grasp did Elizabeth make a move. Then she wrote a diplomatic letter congratulating Mary on her success, before setting off for London with a substantial bodyguard.

In the early months of Mary's reign, Elizabeth was often at her side. The royal sisters made an incongruous pair: Queen Mary, at 37, was small and dark-haired, and dressed in vivid colours with many jewels, while the Lady Elizabeth, at 19, was tall and elegant, and chose to dress very simply in Protestant black and white. The queen had good reasons for keeping Elizabeth close. She longed to convert her sister to the Roman Catholic faith, and – even more importantly – she needed to prevent Elizabeth from becoming a focus for Protestant discontent.

For six months, Elizabeth stayed at court, stubbornly resisting Mary's efforts to compel her to attend the Catholic Mass, but by Christmas she was desperate to leave London and the queen grudgingly granted her request. By this time Mary had started making plans for her marriage to Prince Philip of Spain – to the horror and outrage of many of her subjects, and in January the mood of general discontent became outright rebellion, as a group of Protestant nobles, led by Sir Thomas Wyatt, organized an uprising against the queen. For a few dramatic days it seemed that Mary might lose control of the city of London but eventually the rising was suppressed. All the conspirators were sent to the Tower and forced to confess – and the Lady Elizabeth was implicated in their plot. It emerged that the conspirators had intended to replace Mary with her Protestant sister, and had even planned that Elizabeth should marry Edward Courtney, one of the perpetrators of the uprising. But the important question was: did Elizabeth know and approve of their plans? Wyatt admitted writing a letter to Elizabeth warning her to stay away from London. It was also known that Sir James Croftes had visited her in Hertfordshire with another warning, but these facts alone were not enough to incriminate Elizabeth in the plot.

Elizabeth had been summoned to court when the rebellion began, and in March she faced a hostile interrogation by Stephen Gardiner, the queen's Lord Chancellor and a ruthless political operator. When Gardiner's cross-questioning failed to produce any results, the Royal Council resolved to transfer Elizabeth to the Tower of London, and on 18 March, she was taken by barge to the terrifying prison where her mother had been held eighteen years before. As she passed through the Tower's grim entrance gate, Elizabeth must have wondered whether she would ever emerge alive.

For three months, Elizabeth was held prisoner in the Tower while the cross-examination continued, and all that time she faced the very real prospect of execution

YOUNG ELIZABETH

for treason. Elizabeth later described her imprisonment in the Tower as the most traumatic event of her youth, recalling that 'I stood in danger of my life; my sister was so incensed against me.' Eventually, however, it was decided that such close confinement was no longer needed, and on 19 May she left the Tower in the custody of her gaoler, Sir Henry Bedingfield. Elizabeth's destination was the royal palace at Woodstock, close to Oxford, and the journey took four days. All along the route, people gathered to watch her carriage pass, offering her cakes and calling out loudly 'God save your Grace!'

Woodstock Palace had been a royal hunting lodge since Saxon times, but by the 16th century it was a crumbling ruin. It was also isolated and remote – the perfect place to keep Elizabeth well away from plotters against the queen. Faced with the prospect of an indefinite stay, Elizabeth became petulant and demanding. She waged constant battles with Bedingfield over what books she was allowed, which servants should attend her, and the extent of her walks in the grounds, and she frequently fell ill. But throughout her time at Woodstock, Elizabeth remained determined to assert her innocence. Elizabeth's period in custody was to leave indelible marks on her character. In later life, she frequently referred to her imprisonment, and she came to believe that she had been rescued from death through God's special will, so that she could fulfil his purpose of becoming a great English queen.

Elizabeth's house arrest at Woodstock finally came to an end in March 1555. After ten months of exile, public sympathy for Elizabeth was gathering momentum, and the Royal Council decided it would be safer to keep her under surveillance at court. There were other reasons too for relaxing security. By this time Queen Mary had married Philip of Spain and was believed to be pregnant. With the imminent prospect of a royal heir, Elizabeth no longer posed such a serious threat to the crown. In the event, however, Mary's pregnancy proved to be an illusion. Following the discovery of Mary's self-deception, it seemed there was little chance of the queen ever bearing a child. Even her husband Philip began to pay attention to Elizabeth, as the most likely successor to the English throne.

Mary reigned for three and a half more years after Elizabeth's return from Woodstock. During this period, she pursued a determined campaign to wipe out Protestantism in England, consigning hundreds of men and women to death by burning. As Mary's reign of terror continued, many people longed for a change of monarch, but Elizabeth was careful never to encourage disloyalty to the crown. In the autumn of 1558, however, Mary became seriously ill, and on 17 November 1558 she died, at the age of 42. Elizabeth's moment had arrived.

Hail to the Queen

Elizabeth was reading underneath a tree in Hatfield Park when she was brought the news of her accession to the throne. Dropping to her knees she gave thanks to God, 'This is the lord's doing: it is marvellous in our eyes.' Later that day, she summoned a meeting of her councillors to discuss immediate plans. There would be three days of mourning for Queen Mary. In the meantime, Elizabeth would get to work on the urgent task of forming her Royal Council.

Among the queen's first appointments was Sir William Cecil as secretary of state. The 38-year-old Cecil had already served as chief minister to the young King Edward, and had proved himself to be hardworking, discreet and trustworthy. Unusually for a Tudor politician, Cecil was always prepared to put the interests of his country above his own ambitions and he was to serve Elizabeth faithfully until his death at the age of 76. In her personal household, all Elizabeth's faithful servants stayed in place, with Kat Ashley becoming first lady of the bedchamber. Elizabeth was famously concerned with appearances, and no one who was ugly stood a chance of employment in her household. But to her chosen servants she showed great kindness and loyalty, even making sure that they were cared for when they became old and sick.

On 28 November, Elizabeth arrived at the Tower of London – the traditional waiting place for English monarchs in the weeks leading up to their coronations. Dressed in purple velvet and flanked by courtiers, she was greeted by rapturous cheers, pealing of bells, fanfares of trumpets and a volley of guns lasting for half an hour. It seemed that the whole of London had gathered to see their new queen, and the crowds were not disappointed. In particular, people remarked on the young queen's evident interest in her subjects and her 'stately stooping to the meanest sort'. And this was just the beginning of the royal show. On 14 January, the day before her coronation, Elizabeth embarked on a four-hour 'progress' though the city of London, seated in an open litter and dressed in a robe of gold and silver cloth, trimmed with ermine. Even more spectacular was the procession the following day, conveying Elizabeth to Westminster Abbey, while the coronation was followed by a celebration banquet lasting from three in the afternoon until one the following morning.

It was a truly magnificent start to a reign that would soon become famous for its style and display.

Dr John Dee: The Queen's Magician

In the opening weeks of her reign, Elizabeth consulted Dr John Dee on the most auspicious date for her coronation. Drawing on his extensive knowledge of astrology, he settled on Sunday 15 January. Dee was one of the most outstanding scholars of the Elizabethan age, but also one of its most controversial figures. An expert in mathematics, astronomy and navigation, he also practised the arcane art of alchemy and devoted most of his later life to investigating the occult and supernatural. Dee acted as an astrological and scientific adviser to Elizabeth and her court, helped her captains to plan their voyages of discovery, and was a passionate advocate for the establishment of English colonies in the New World. In the closing years of his life, he faced personal ruin and sought support from Elizabeth, who made him Warden of Christ's College in Manchester.

Elizabeth's Suitors

Elizabeth was greeted rapturously as queen. But one question hung over her: who would the queen choose as her husband? It was taken for granted that a young woman could not rule alone, and there was a pressing need for an heir to the throne. Ever since the reign of Henry VIII, the Tudors had been dogged by problems of succession and now the situation was even more urgent. With no direct heir, two contenders for the English throne had emerged. One was Lady Katherine Grey, King Henry's great-niece through his younger sister Mary, and younger sister of Jane, the nine days' queen. The other was Mary Stuart, Queen of Scots, also a great-niece of King Henry's through his older sister Margaret. Both these young women were Roman Catholics and both had connections with foreign powers. Although brought up as a Protestant, Katherine Grey had converted to Catholicism during Edward's reign and had established strong links with Spain, while Mary, Queen of Scots was part of the French royal family through her marriage to the French dauphin. To English Protestants, the young Queen Elizabeth's position looked worryingly insecure.

It was clear that Elizabeth had to marry and produce an heir, but the choice of a suitable husband was not straightforward. If she chose from among the great ruling families of Europe – as befitted her royal status – she ran the risk of delivering England into foreign hands. However, if she decided to wed a member of the English nobility, her choice could result in civil war as rival noblemen raised objections. Elizabeth had seen how deeply unpopular Queen Mary's Spanish marriage had made her in England and she resolved not to make the same mistake. On the other hand, it was distracting and enjoyable to see what offers of marriage she might receive.

The young Elizabeth was beautiful, intelligent and charming – and suitors came flocking to pay court to the most eligible lady in Europe. In January 1559, the Spanish ambassador informed the queen of the hopes of King Philip II, and Elizabeth responded with typical prevarication. On the one hand, she proclaimed her choice to remain a Virgin Queen while also protesting that she was prevented by law from marrying the husband of her half-sister. On the other hand, she promised to lay the matter before Parliament, assuring Philip that if she married at all, she would prefer him above all others. Elizabeth was a consummate politician and she realized that it would not be wise to turn down one of Europe's most powerful men with unflattering haste.

Philip II was not the only suitor encouraged by Elizabeth that winter. In February, an ambassador from the court of the Holy Roman Emperor, Ferdinand I, arrived in England. His apparent purpose was to present his master's compliments to the queen, but he was really inquiring about the marriage prospects of the emperor's two sons, the Archdukes Ferdinand and Charles. Elizabeth dismissed the excessively pious Ferdinand as 'fit only for praying' but expressed an

The Queen's Progress

Throughout her reign, Queen Elizabeth undertook journeys, or progresses, around her kingdom. These royal progresses, which generally took place in the summer, allowed the queen to see her subjects and to be seen, and also served the purpose of keeping her out of London during the plague season. At each stage of her route, the queen stayed in the home of an aristocrat, where she expected to be entertained in style. On a typical progress, Elizabeth was accompanied by at least a hundred members of her household – all of whom had to be housed and fed.

An account from the year 1564 describes a royal progress that stopped five days in Cambridge. The queen entered the city gates preceded by trumpets and followed by her magnificent retinue, where she was welcomed by all the scholars of the university, kneeling and calling out 'Vivat Regina!' For the next five days, the queen was entertained by a series of ceremonies, entertainments and 'scholastic exercises'. She visited the colleges founded by members of the Tudor family, attended lectures and Latin plays, listened to orations and disputes and was presented with numerous gifts. She also gave several speeches of her own in Latin. When she finally left, one day later than planned, she said she would have stayed even longer 'if provision of beer and ale' could have been made for her court.

interest in Charles, insisting, however, that she must first see him with her own eyes. Questioning the imperial ambassador closely, she inquired whether it was true that Charles had a head too large for his body. While the ambassador vehemently proclaimed Charles' suitability as a royal husband, he refused to agree to a humiliating visit 'on approval'.

In April, Prince Erik of Sweden joined the ranks of the queen's suitors. He had pursued Elizabeth during Mary's reign and now he redoubled his efforts, showering the queen with gifts of furs and tapestries and writing her passionate love letters. Elizabeth was charmed by

Why Did Elizabeth Refuse To Marry?

Within three years of Elizabeth's accession it had become painfully clear that while she enjoyed the game of flirting and accepting compliments, she was disinclined to take a husband. But what were the reasons underlying Elizabeth's choice to stay single? Some historians have suggested that she was traumatized by her early sexual encounters with Thomas Seymour, citing her comment to a Scots envoy in 1561 that 'certain events in her youth' had made it impossible for her to equate marriage with security. Some have hazarded – as many of her contemporaries did – that Elizabeth knew she was infertile or otherwise unsuited for married life. It was also possible that she was so in love with Robert Dudley that she could not accept any other man as her husband. But perhaps the most likely reason for her adoption of the role of Virgin Queen was the simple fact that Elizabeth liked to have her own way. Recognizing that any husband would expect to rule, she preferred to stay single and govern her kingdom as she chose.

portraits of the prince but she refused his demand that she should live in Sweden as his wife. Meanwhile representatives of the dukes of Saxony and Holstein also brought offers of marriage, to which Elizabeth withheld her response for as long as she possibly could.

Within a court crowded with foreign ambassadors, some hopeful Englishmen were also pressing their suit. Sir Henry Fitzalan was a fabulously rich buffoon, who lived in King Henry's old palace at Nonsuch. While Elizabeth had no romantic interest in him at all, she nevertheless enjoyed stringing him along. A more serious contender for the queen's affections was the handsome and charming diplomat Sir William Pickering, and Elizabeth amused herself by flirting with him. But in reality there was only one English nobleman who could ever lay claim to Elizabeth's heart – and his name was Robert Dudley.

'Bonny Sweet Robin'

Elizabeth had known her 'bonny sweet Robin' (as she

called him) since she was 8 years old and counted him as one of her oldest and dearest friends. He had grown up at court and was a natural choice for the select group of aristocratic children who shared their lessons with Elizabeth and Edward. As the son of the powerful Duke of Northumberland, he belonged to one of the leading families in the land, but in fact the Dudleys had a chequered history, with two generations executed for treason (Edmund Dudley, Henry Tudor's despised tax collector, had been put to death by Henry VIII, while Robert's father, John Dudley, faced execution for attempting to place Lady Jane Grey on the throne). After the deposition of Lady Jane Grey, Robert Dudley himself had been condemned to death, before being pardoned with the help of King Philip II of Spain. Elizabeth liked to tease her friend that he came from a family of traitors.

In the young Robert Dudley, Elizabeth found a fellow spirit. Intelligent, charming, handsome and brave, he was also a superb horseman and sportsman. One of her first decisions as queen was to elect Dudley as her Master of the Horse, a position that involved co-ordinating royal events and riding beside her in processions. But Dudley was not just seen at the queen's side at public events. Within the court he had more access to Elizabeth than any of her councillors and rumours about their intimate relationship were rife. Among his fellow peers, Dudley was regarded with great suspicion and William Cecil was especially fearful of his influence over the queen. However, there was one major obstacle in the way of Dudley's relationship with Elizabeth. He was married to a lady called Amy Robsart, and although his wife was reported to have 'a malady in one of her breasts', her continued existence, living quietly in the country, prevented the royal affair from progressing any further.

In 1560, however, Dudley's situation changed, when his wife was discovered lying at the base of a flight of steps in her house in Oxfordshire. Amy's neck was broken and foul play was suspected. Naturally the finger of suspicion pointed at her husband and Elizabeth was alarmed. Anxious to deflect guilt from her favourite, the queen immediately ordered an enquiry, but although a verdict of accidental death was returned, Dudley was left with a damaging slur on his reputation. Even after Amy's mysterious death, Elizabeth still appeared to nurse the hope that she and Dudley might marry, and Dudley remained a constant presence at court, infuriating all her other councillors by his privileged access to the queen.

The Question of Succession

Soon after Elizabeth's 29th birthday, the succession question acquired a sudden urgency. The queen was at Hampton Court when she began to run a high fever and smallpox was diagnosed. Within a couple of days, she had lapsed into a coma, in which she remained for the next 48 hours. As the queen lay drifting in and out of consciousness, the Privy Council held urgent debates on who should be offered the crown in the event of her death. One group favoured Lady Katherine Grey, younger sister of the ill-fated Jane, while another supported the Earl of Huntingdon, a descendant of Edward II, with no close blood links to Elizabeth. Nobody mentioned the name of Mary, Queen of Scots.

Eventually, Elizabeth rallied. Aware that she was still dangerously ill, she appointed Robert Dudley as Lord Protector of England. Her councillors agreed to everything she asked, anxious not to distress their queen who was 'all but gone', but privately they agreed that such an appointment would lead to civil war. From then on, Elizabeth began a slow recovery, much to the relief of her councillors and subjects. But the crisis had provided a worrying glimpse of the chaos that could follow if the queen persisted in refusing to name her heir. When Parliament met in January 1563, the Lords and the Commons urged their sovereign to marry and produce an heir, but Elizabeth once again resisted all pressure.

While Elizabeth refused to name her heir, attention inevitably focused on Lady Katherine Grey. She was the beauty of the family, and an ambitious young woman who had enlisted the support of successive Spanish ambassadors in her claim to the throne. There had even been a secret plan to marry her to King Philip's son and set the pair on the English throne. But Katherine had wrecked this scheme by falling in love with Edward Seymour (son of the Lord Protector during the reign of King Edward VI). After her secret marriage to Seymour, Katherine continued to serve as one of the queen's ladies of the bedchamber, but when she became pregnant, in 1561, her secret was revealed. Elizabeth was furious – both at Katherine's lack of sense and her defiance of royal authority (it was against the law for persons of royal blood to marry without the sovereign's consent). In Elizabeth's view, Katherine's weakness in following her romantic instincts made her entirely unsuitable to inherit the throne.

In August, Lady Katherine Grey was imprisoned in the Tower of London, while her husband was housed in a separate cell, and in September she gave birth to a son. News of a possible new claimant to the throne incensed the queen even further, and she gave orders for a commission to investigate the validity of Katherine's marriage. The commission discovered that Katherine could produce no evidence of her wedding, and in 1562 her union was pronounced null and void and her heir illegitimate. The immediate threat of a rival claim to the throne had been snuffed out, and Katherine remained imprisoned in the Tower.

The drama had a sequel the following year when Katherine gave birth to a second son, and it emerged that her gaolers had allowed her to meet clandestinely with her husband. This time the couple were strictly separated and Katherine spent the rest of her life under close surveillance, eventually dying of tuberculosis in 1568. Meanwhile, her sons were placed in the care of William Cecil, who brought them up for a time with his own children.

Matters of State

While the ever-pressing questions of marriage and

succession dominated the first half of Elizabeth's reign, there were other urgent matters demanding her attention. As a new young monarch, she had inherited a kingdom with many problems. By the end of Mary's reign, poverty and lawlessness were rife. In the country, wealthy landowners were pursuing a ruthless policy of enclosure, claiming common land from the poor. Meanwhile the English towns were filling up with beggars, including the homeless monks and nuns who had once provided succour to the poor. Under Queen Mary, foreign trade had declined and Mary's government had also fallen into debt, to the tune of £266,000 – a shockingly high figure for Tudor times. Most worrying of all, the English people were deeply divided on matters of religion, and an atmosphere of fear and suspicion reigned in the wake of Mary's savage religious persecutions.

Elizabeth's first priority was to re-establish the Church of England as her country's lawful religion, and in April 1599 Parliament passed two very important acts. The Act of Supremacy asserted Elizabeth's right to be Supreme Governor of the English Church, while the Act of Uniformity restored Edward VI's *Book of Common Prayer,* decreeing that all services should be conducted in English and outlawing the Catholic Mass. With the passing of these two acts (sometimes known as the Anglican Settlement), Elizabeth had returned England to its position before Mary's reign, as a Protestant country with the monarch at its head. Now she proceeded with tolerance and caution. Under Elizabeth, there was no religious persecution. She discouraged religious fanaticism of any kind, and actively banned the preaching of contentious sermons. While the Act of Uniformity insisted that every subject over 16 had to attend church on Sundays and enforced a fine of 12 pence for non-attendance, there were no attempts to force people to change their beliefs and the queen turned a blind eye to the celebration of Mass in private. Catholics were welcomed at court, with the expectation that they would be discreet about their beliefs, and the queen sometimes stayed in the homes of the Catholic nobility. The queen's own preference was for a relaxed form of Protestantism that retained some of the music and ritual of the old faith, and while her government banned the veneration of saints, she actively encouraged the cult of St George, England's national saint.

On the matter of finances, Elizabeth addressed herself seriously to the task of reducing her government's debt. Determined to live within her means, she set about selling off crown lands and making economies at court. While she never stinted on money for costumes and jewels, she nevertheless watched her finances carefully, and deliberately cut down on her number of royal progresses. On the national stage, she continued the reforms to the English coinage begun in Mary's reign, as her government called in all debased coins and replaced them with new currency containing the correct proportions of gold or silver. Elizabeth also encouraged the development of trade, reducing some of the heavy taxes that Mary had imposed on English merchants. Her reign saw a steady influx of Protestant refugees from Europe, and these new communities provided a valuable boost to English industry, introducing skills such as lace making, silk weaving and engraving.

Concerns about expense also dominated Elizabeth's approach to foreign policy, and in the early years of her reign she refused all temptations to engage in costly foreign wars – with just one exception. Ever since Queen Mary had lost Calais in 1558, the English had been desperate to regain a territory that they saw as part of England, and in 1562 Elizabeth believed that she had the chance to win it back. War had broken out in France between the Catholics and the Protestant Huguenots, and Elizabeth pledged help to the Huguenots in return for their support in recapturing Calais.

In October 1562, 6,000 men sailed to Newhaven (later renamed Le Havre) under the command of Ambrose Dudley, Earl of Warwick – Robert Dudley's brother. Their role was to reinforce the Huguenot armies, but by March

1563 the French wars had come to an end, rendering the English troops redundant. Instead of recalling her men, however, Elizabeth insisted that they stay on in Le Havre, where they faced the combined assault of Catholic and Huguenot armies, coupled with a terrible epidemic of plague. In July Elizabeth reluctantly agreed that Warwick had no choice but to surrender Le Havre to the French, and the following spring she signed the Peace of Troyes with France, in which England finally renounced all claims to Calais.

After her disastrous French campaign, Elizabeth did not venture any English troops abroad for more than 20 years. However, she did pursue an aggressive policy against the wealth and power of Spain. King Philip II of Spain was fabulously wealthy, thanks to the riches of the New World, and Elizabeth was determined not to let the Spanish monopoly go unchallenged. By the 1560s, she was sponsoring Captain John Hawkins to undertake trading voyages to the Americas, in which he established trading deals with the natives, and also indulged in some raiding of Spanish merchant ships. It was a risky policy, bringing rich rewards, but also incurring the wrath of the Spanish sovereign. Even in the early years of her reign, Elizabeth was already sowing the seeds for her great confrontation with Spain.

Dangerous Mary

From the earliest days of her reign, Elizabeth was plagued by the problem of her cousin Mary Stuart. Mary had inherited the title of Queen of the Scots when she was just 6 days old, and had married the heir to the French throne at the age of 15. Following the death of King Francis II in 1559 (the year after Elizabeth was crowned queen), Mary had become queen consort of France as well as Mary, Queen of Scots, and she and her young husband had insisted on styling themselves monarchs of France, Scotland and England.

In 1560, Mary was suddenly widowed, and the following year, aged 18, she moved back to Scotland where she began to rule in her own right, attempting to exert a precarious control over the powerful Protestant lords at court. While Mary was no longer queen in France, she nevertheless posed a serious threat to England's security, maintaining close links with the French crown, and persisting in her claim that she was the true Catholic inheritor of the English throne.

At this stage, Queen Elizabeth decided it was time to open negotiations with her royal cousin. Elizabeth's government was desperate for Mary to ratify the Treaty of Edinburgh. This was an agreement that had been drawn up with the old French king by which France undertook to withdraw troops from Scotland and recognize Elizabeth's right to rule England. However, Mary had never agreed to sign the document, and now she prevaricated infuriatingly. Elizabeth, for her part, refused to confirm that Mary would succeed her as queen of England in the event of her death – and a delicate impasse developed between the two young rulers.

Between 1561 and 1565, Mary and Elizabeth made tentative plans to meet, exchanging affectionate letters and messages. Elizabeth clearly felt an affinity with Mary as another young female monarch surrounded by ambitious men. Elizabeth also took a close interest in Mary's marriage plans (a matter of great relevance to her kingdom's security) and by 1563 she was promoting the suit of Lord Robert Dudley. Mary was justly suspicious – Dudley was not only the queen's great favourite but he was also a devout Protestant. Marriage to him would clearly provide Elizabeth with a means of controlling her.

Mary was notoriously impulsive in matters of the heart, and in July 1565 she took a step that would eventually cost her the Scottish crown. Defying the advice of the powerful Scottish Protestant lords, she married the 19-year-old Lord Henry Darnley, a noble with his own claim to the English throne (Darnley and Mary shared a grandmother – Henry VIII's sister, Margaret Tudor). Elizabeth was furious that Mary should make a marriage so 'perilous to the amity between the queens of both the realms'. She was also confident that Darnley would soon show his true colours as a vain, ambitious and bullying young man. And it was not long before Mary realized her terrible mistake. By December, when it was announced that the Scottish queen was pregnant, the couple were already living apart, with Mary seeking out the company of her Italian secretary David Rizzio. Wild with jealousy at Rizzio's influence, Darnley entered into a conspiracy to murder Rizzio and in July 1566 stabbed him to death. However, within twelve months, Darnley was himself the victim of an assassination plot. On the evening of 10 February 1567, there was a sudden explosion at the house where he was staying. Darnley's body was found amidst the rubble and foul play was evident.

On hearing of the shocking events in Scotland, Elizabeth wrote immediately to Mary, urging her to waste no time in finding his murderers and clearing her name. It was wise advice, but Mary was not to be hurried. By this time she had fallen under the spell of one of the chief suspects in the murder conspiracy, the Protestant Earl of Bothwell, James Hepburn, a man of rash and unpredictable character, with a burning ambition to be king of the Scots.

In April 1567, Mary was returning from a visit to her infant son, Prince James, who had been born ten months earlier. As she rode towards Edinburgh, she was abducted by Bothwell and carried off to his castle, where he 'ravished' her, forcing her to marry him to safeguard her honour. When the news of the queen's latest marriage leaked out, there was outrage in Scotland. While Darnley had been unpopular with the Scottish Protestant lords, Bothwell was loathed, and Mary was widely reviled as a whore. By the end of June the queen was imprisoned in the fortress of Lochleven and Bothwell had fled abroad. On 24 July 1567, Mary was forced to abdicate. Her infant son was crowned King James VI of Scotland.

Over the border in England, Elizabeth was horrified by

the news. Outraged that the Scottish lords should dare to take their monarch prisoner, she resolved to help Mary regain her crown – despite her many misgivings about her cousin's character. However, before Elizabeth had time to take action, Mary had escaped from Lochleven and fled over the border, seeking the protection of the English queen. Elizabeth responded by placing Mary in honourable protective custody, not as a prisoner but as her 'guest': a temporary solution, which would in fact persist for the next nineteen years.

Within four months of Mary's arrival in England, Elizabeth had set up an official enquiry to investigate Darnley's murder. Her motives for this were clearly political: she needed to be sure of the Scottish queen's legal position before she could take any action to help her. If Mary were proved guilty of involvement in the murder plot, she could be sent back to Scotland to face justice. If she were proved innocent, Elizabeth could help to restore her to the Scottish throne. And even if an unclear verdict were returned, Elizabeth would at least be confirmed in her decision to keep her royal cousin in 'honourable captivity'. In the event, the third option prevailed as the enquiry returned a verdict of 'not proven'. A question mark remained over the extent of Mary's guilt and Elizabeth began to make plans for Mary's long-term confinement under the care of George Talbot, Earl of Shrewsbury, and his indomitable wife, Bess of Hardwick.

Revolt Against The Queen

Through no fault of her own, Elizabeth had been placed in an impossible situation. It was clear that Mary needed to be kept under guard. She had never abandoned her claim to the English throne, and, as a free woman on the loose in England, she would have provided a dangerous rallying point for Catholic rebels. Nevertheless, by the simple act of keeping her cousin prisoner, Elizabeth appeared in the eyes of many of her subjects to be a harsh and unfeeling captor. The longer Mary remained a prisoner, the greater her status grew as a romantic martyr. So it was inevitable that she should provide a focus for any serious opposition to Elizabeth.

The first rebellion came in 1569. Later known as the Rising of the North, it was led by two powerful Catholic lords, Charles Neville, Earl of Westmorland, and Thomas Percy, Earl of Northumberland. Both lords were fierce opponents of William Cecil, and both felt cut off from the seat of power in London. They were soon joined by a group of more radical Catholics, who had taken part in the Pilgrimage of Grace against King Henry VIII. The immediate aim of the rebels was to release Mary, Queen of Scots from Tutbury Castle in Staffordshire, while their unstated plan was to set her on the English throne.

In November 1569, the rebels occupied Durham Cathedral, celebrating a Catholic Mass in direct defiance of Elizabeth's Act of Uniformity. Then they advanced towards Tutbury. At first the rebels numbered nearly 10,000, but as they moved southwards, they began to lose momentum, and by 25 November (the day that Mary was moved away from Tutbury), they had begun to retreat. As a final act of defiance they captured Barnard Castle, but were unable to hold onto it, and were easily vanquished by the queen's forces arriving from the south. Pursued by royal armies, the rebel earls fled northward, dispersing their forces and escaping into Scotland.

The Rising of the North had proved easy enough for Elizabeth to contain, but there was a worrying sequel in January 1570, when a member of the powerful Dacre family rose in revolt against the queen. From his base in Cumbria, Leonard Dacre rallied a number of sympathetic Scottish nobles, who might have formed a dangerous invasion force. However, the threat was contained by Elizabeth's cousin, Baron Henry Hunsdon, who managed to annihilate Dacre's army before he could be joined by his Scottish allies. Realizing his revolt was doomed, Dacre fled into exile in Flanders.

The rebellions in the north did no long-term damage to Elizabeth. Life in southern England continued unaffected, while the northern troubles gave her the chance to strengthen royal control in the region. In the months following the Rising of the North, there were hundreds of executions and many large confiscations of property, with the result that the massive estates of the Percy, Neville and Dacre families were effectively dismantled. By rising up in protest against their sovereign, the rebel northern lords had in fact provided her with the perfect opportunity to bring them firmly under royal control.

The northern uprisings had one serious consequence for Elizabeth's security. While they were planning their revolt, the Catholic lords were troubled by the fear that they would be committing a sin by rebelling against their lawful ruler. So, on the eve of their uprising they petitioned Pope Pius V to assist in their struggle. The pope's response came too late to provide any practical help, but it was unequivocal in its support for a Catholic rebellion. In February 1570, Pope Pius issued a Papal Bull officially excommunicating Elizabeth, and threatening those Catholics who obeyed her with excommunication. The pope had seen his chance to replace a troublesome Protestant queen with her Catholic cousin and he was offering open encouragement to any future plots against Elizabeth.

By the year 1570, Elizabeth had been queen for 11 years, but the issues of her marriage and successor had still not been resolved. As she approached her 37th birthday, it was clearly urgent that she should marry soon if she were to stand a chance of producing an heir. Many of her subjects, however, had resigned themselves to the prospect of being ruled by a Virgin Queen. After the turmoil of the previous two reigns, Elizabeth had proved herself to be a competent monarch, presiding over a period of peace and religious tolerance. She had found a way of working with her council, relying mainly on William Cecil's advice. In her dealings with Mary, the chief rival to her throne, she had been firm but fair, and she had survived several uprisings with her royal authority intact. Elizabeth had also managed to retain the loyalty of most of her subjects, who viewed their queen with affection and respect.

Chapter 8
THE END OF THE DYNASTY – GLORIANA

Queen Elizabeth's response to her excommunication was a defiant one: she granted the people of England a holiday. In 1570, she declared 17 November to be Accession Day, also known as Queen Day, to celebrate her accession to the throne twelve years earlier. The annual holiday was an official holy day of the newly established Church and was celebrated by tilting, poetry, pageantry and music. The nobles and gentlemen who broke their lances in her honour arrived in the lists in fancy dress and made speeches, weaving a romantic story around their attire as a compliment to the queen. Thousands turned out to witness the spectacle.

As Elizabeth's reign advanced, Accession Day became a major event in the English calendar, designed to promote the cult of their Virgin Queen. In pageants, poems and paintings, Elizabeth would appear in the form of Astrea, the virgin goddess of justice, Diana, the huntress, Cynthia, the lady of the sea, and, in later years, as Gloriana, the Faerie Queen – an invention of the poet Edmund Spenser. In all these roles, Elizabeth was surrounded by a host of adoring knights, ready to sacrifice their lives in her service.

Elizabeth was flattered and delighted by these elaborate tributes, but what mattered most of all to her was the love of her subjects. In her public speeches and proclamations she constantly reminded the English people that she was like a mother to all of them, deeply concerned for their 'safety and quietness'. She made it a point of principle to appear in public as much as possible, riding through the streets, being rowed in her royal barge, and travelling on annual progresses through her kingdom. And wherever she went, she always had time to stop and talk to her subjects, graciously receiving their gifts and listening to their petitions. In the words of Sir Walter Raleigh 'she was the Queen of the small as well as the great and she would hear their complaints'.

Mary the Rival Queen

In fact, Elizabeth's throne was far from secure in 1570.

Ever since the summer of 1568, Mary, Queen of Scots had been held in honourable captivity in England, while negotiations were held to return her to the Scottish throne. But she was a dangerous hostage and in 1570 she became the focus of an international conspiracy against Elizabeth. The plotting began when a Florentine banker named Roberto Ridolfi wrote to the Bishop of Ross, Mary's ambassador to Elizabeth, outlining plans for the invasion of England by the Duke of Alba, head of the Spanish forces in the Netherlands, with the backing of the pope and Philip II of Spain. The invaders aimed to foment another uprising among the nobility in the north and their Catholic sympathizers. Thomas Howard, Duke of Norfolk was then to arrest Elizabeth, marry Mary and put her on the throne. It was a dangerous plot, combining many forces, at home and abroad, but it did not succeed. Elizabeth's spy network got wind of it and the ringleaders were rounded up and arrested. Norfolk was eventually executed for treason in 1572. Ridolfi himself was abroad at the time of the plot's discovery and so he escaped punishment.

As the disturbing facts of the Ridolfi conspiracy were uncovered, it became evident that Mary had not only known about the plot, but had encouraged it. Many people in England saw Mary's involvement as outright treason, and Parliament called for her execution. However, Elizabeth flatly refused to contemplate such a punishment, stating that she could never 'put to death the bird that, to escape the pursuit of the hawk, has fled to my feet for protection'. Nevertheless, the Ridolfi plot did have the result of hardening Elizabeth's attitude to her cousin. Resolving that Mary should never again sit on the Scottish throne, she finally recognized Mary's son, James VI, as the rightful king of the Scots.

With the drama of the Ridolfi conspiracy behind her, Mary faced the prospect of a lifetime of captivity. She passed her time in reading, prayer and embroidery, rapidly acquiring the status of a martyr, while discontented Catholics continued to dream of placing her on the English throne. In 1583, she was implicated in a plot orchestrated by Francis Throckmorton, a Catholic English nobleman. The conspirators planned that the French Duc de Guise would invade England with Spanish support to put Mary on the throne and restore the Catholic faith. But the plot was discovered by Sir Francis Walsingham, Elizabeth's spymaster. Throckmorton was arrested, tortured and executed in 1584. Once again disaster had been averted, but the danger posed by Mary refused to go away.

In 1586, Elizabeth was threatened by another potentially deadly plot. This time Philip II of Spain was directly involved, as he set in motion new plans to invade England. In negotiations with the pope, Philip agreed to put Mary on the throne, with a husband and successor of his choice. Meanwhile, in England, Sir Anthony Babington, a covert Catholic, led a plot against Elizabeth. Babington aimed to encourage a rising by English Catholics to assassinate Elizabeth, and Philip promised to send an invasion force as soon as the queen was dead. Babington wrote to Mary telling her of his plans, but his letters and her replies were intercepted and deciphered by Walsingham. When Babington realized that the plot had been discovered, he fled, but he was caught, tried for high treason and sentenced to death.

Everybody recognized that the Babington plot had seriously endangered both the life of the queen and the peace and stability of her country. There was also no denying that Mary had been involved in this plot against Elizabeth. Parliament demanded that Mary should be brought to trial and Elizabeth reluctantly agreed. In October 1586, Mary stood trial at Fotheringhay Castle in Northamptonshire. She was condemned for her part in the assassination plot, and a sentence of execution was passed. But one more step had to be taken before Mary could meet her death: Elizabeth had to sign the death warrant. It took three months for Elizabeth to put her name to the fatal document and it was one of the hardest decisions of her reign. While she recognized that Mary had become too dangerous to stay alive, she still shrunk from condemning an anointed queen to death and spilling the blood of her cousin. Eventually, however, the warrant was signed and Mary was executed on 8 February 1587. When the news of her death reached London, the crowds went wild with joy – bells were rung, guns were fired and bonfires were lit. But Elizabeth did not share in the general rejoicing. She spent the day alone, weeping and refusing all food.

Wooing the Queen

Elizabeth never tired of compliments from handsome men. Right up until the end of her reign, she still had her favourites at court – charming, talented men who knew how to flatter her, but who also offered her friendship and advice. Robert Dudley, to whom she had been so close during her youth, remained chief among these favourites and she granted him the title of the Earl of Leicester in 1564. Leicester never abandoned his devotion to the queen, but as they both entered their forties, their relationship came to resemble that of a long-married couple, filled with affection and gentle banter. Yet there could still be storms between them at times. When Leicester finally married again, at the age of 46, Elizabeth sulked for weeks and banished his wife from her court. When he died ten years later she was heartbroken. Other notable favourites in Elizabeth's later years were Sir Christopher Hatton, the Earl of Oxford, and the dashing Sir Walter Raleigh (see panel on page 342), while at the end of her reign the young Earl of Essex captured her heart before repaying her affection with treachery (see pages 366–367).

While Elizabeth enjoyed the attention of her courtiers, she was still receiving foreign offers of marriage. In the early 1570s, marriage negotiations had begun between Francis, Duke of Anjou, brother of the French king, and the English queen. The time was right for England to forge an alliance with France against the growing might of Spain, but Elizabeth had some serious reservations. Anjou was twenty-two years younger than her and she feared such a match would make her look

Sir Francis Walsingham: Elizabeth's Spymaster (1532–90)

Francis Walsingham studied law at Cambridge and in Padua in Italy before becoming a member of parliament in 1559. William Cecil soon recognized his talent for subterfuge and used him to obtain information from foreign spies in London. In 1569, Cecil assigned Walsingham to unravel the Ridolfi plot, his first government role. Twelve years later, Walsingham led the investigation that uncovered the Throckmorton plot to replace Elizabeth with Mary, Queen of Scots. By the 1580s he had developed a network of spies, and was reading all Mary's correspondence. He also sent a double agent to offer Mary a secret channel of communication. At the time of the Babington plot, Mary was being held at Chartley in Staffordshire. Coded notes, passed in and out in beer barrels, were all deciphered in Walsingham's office. As soon as Walsingham saw Babington's letter outlining his plot, he forwarded it to Mary in the hope that she would make a compromising reply. When she did, she had sealed her fate.

In addition to his role as a spymaster, Walsingham was one of Elizabeth's chief advisers. He became her principal secretary in 1573 and was knighted in 1577. In foreign affairs, he counselled against Elizabeth's marriage to Duke Francis of Anjou and worked hard to strengthen England's defences against the Spanish Armada. He encouraged Elizabeth to give support to the French Huguenots in their struggle against the Catholics and promoted trade and exploration.

ridiculous. He was also said to be extremely small and badly disfigured by smallpox scars. However, these objections were set aside in 1578, when the Duke of Anjou led an invasion force against the army of Philip of Spain in the Netherlands. As a result of this action, the people of the Netherlands invited Anjou to become their governor, placing him in a key position in relation to the kingdom of England. Recognizing that the Duke of Anjou could be either a useful ally or a dangerous enemy, some members of Elizabeth's council urged

Elizabeth In Love

The Duke of Anjou's visit to England was cut short when he received news of a friend's death in France, and on 29 August 1578, he left Greenwich to travel to Dover. Even before he set sail he had written four letters to Elizabeth and he sent three more when he arrived at Boulogne. In one of these letters he signed himself 'the most faithful and affectionate slave in the world'. Elizabeth, for her part, was devastated by their parting. The historian and writer Alison Weir records that the queen wrote the poem 'On Monsieur's Departure' at this time:

> *I grieve, yet dare not show my discontent;*
> *I love, and yet am forced to seem to hate,*
> *I dote, but dare not what I meant;*
> *I seem stark mute, yet inwardly do prate.*
> *I am, and am not, freeze, and yet I burn,*
> *Since from myself my other self I turn.*

('On Monsieur's Departure', verse 1)

her to consider marriage. Anjou was also eager for the union, as he badly needed funds for his campaigns in the Low Countries.

In autumn 1578 Anjou sent a charming ambassador to England to prepare the queen for his 'frenzied wooing', and the following summer he arrived to pursue his suit himself. On the evening of 17 August, Elizabeth secretly stole out of Greenwich Palace to dine with Anjou and was delighted by what she saw. In place of the disfigured midget she had expected, she saw a confident, bearded young man of about her own height, with great personal charm and evident sex appeal. Apparently the attraction was mutual, and the couple were soon addressing each other in terms of extravagant affection. Elizabeth nicknamed Anjou her 'frog' and they swore to love each other until they were parted by death. By the time they made their tearful parting, after almost two weeks of whirlwind romance, a royal marriage seemed a definite prospect. But with Anjou abroad once more, the queen began to realize the implications of such a union. By marrying the Duke, she would be forced to share her throne with a foreigner and a Catholic, and would risk turmoil and rebellion in her country. Meanwhile, Anjou was still besieging her with passionate love letters and gifts. For almost two years she wavered, sometimes desperate for marriage to her beloved frog, and sometimes resolved against it. Eventually she allowed her head to rule her heart. By the end of 1582, Elizabeth had made it clear that there was no prospect of a marriage, although she was sick at heart. As she told her courtiers sadly, 'I am an old woman to whom pater nosters will suffice in the place of nuptials.'

Pirates and Adventurers

Elizabeth played a more prominent role on the international stage in the second half of her reign. While she still avoided war whenever she could, her sympathies with the Protestants in the Low Countries and France led her to lend military support to their struggles. She was also more than happy to harass King Philip II of Spain through the activities of English sea captains such as John Hawkins and Francis Drake. In the 1570s, these audacious privateers were ruthless in their plunder of Spanish treasure ships on their voyages home from the New World, and even began to attack the ships when they lay in port.

In 1571, Drake led raids against Spanish outposts and ships in the Caribbean, seizing booty worth more than £100,000. The following year, he attacked Panama, scaled the central ridge and saw the Pacific Ocean, which, so far, had been the exclusive domain of the Spaniards. Drake conceived a bold ambition to sail into the Pacific and raid Spanish settlements there and, with the help of Francis Walsingham, he persuaded the queen to invest in his scheme. In November 1577 Drake set sail from Plymouth with just five ships and fewer than 200 men. Although he added to his fleet with Spanish treasure ships taken on his passage across the Atlantic, the weather and disease took a heavy toll. When he passed through the Straits of

Sir Walter Raleigh: Soldier, Explorer, Settler and Courtier (1552–1618)

Walter Raleigh was an aristocratic soldier and sea captain who came to the attention of Queen Elizabeth in 1580, when he went to Ireland to help suppress an uprising in Munster. He soon became a favourite at court, and was knighted in 1585. In the same year he sailed to America and founded the first English colony on Roanoke Island (now North Carolina). Raleigh named the colony Virginia in honour of the Virgin Queen. However, he never set foot there himself and the settlement was a failure. In 1587, Raleigh sent a second expedition and left another group of settlers, but this group, like the first, did not survive. Raleigh has been credited with bringing the first potatoes and tobacco to England, although both of these had already been introduced by Spanish traders. However, he did help to make smoking popular at court.

In 1592, the queen discovered Raleigh's secret marriage to one of her maids of honour, and briefly imprisoned Raleigh and his wife in the Tower. He later attempted to regain royal favour by setting off to find El Dorado, the fabled 'Golden Land' rumoured to be situated somewhere beyond the mouth of the Orinoco river in Guiana (now Venezuela). However, the expedition was not a success.

When James I came to the throne in 1603, Raleigh fell from favour and he was imprisoned in the Tower accused of plotting against the king. Following his release in 1616, he defied royal orders and, while leading a further expedition to South America, he launched an attack on a Spanish settlement. Raleigh was arrested on his return to England and was beheaded in 1618.

Magellan into the Pacific the following September, only one ship remained – the 100-ton *Golden Hind*.

After pillaging Spanish settlements and coastal shipping, Drake set off to explore further up the western coast of North America, hoping to find a northwest passage back to England. Defeated by the cold as he travelled northwards, he turned south again and anchored just north of the site of modern San Francisco, naming the land there New Albion and claiming it for Queen Elizabeth. He then set sail westwards across the Pacific Ocean and returned home via the Indian Ocean and the Cape of Good Hope. On his return to England, Drake was feted as the first Englishman to circumnavigate the globe.

Drake arrived back in Plymouth on 26 September 1580. When the *Golden Hind* docked in Deptford the following April, Queen Elizabeth came on board and knighted Drake, recognizing him as a national hero, despite protests from Spain. Drake's famous voyage had brought wealth as well as glory to England. His remaining crew shared £40,000, while he took an extra £10,000. The investors in the voyage doubled their money and the rest of the vast haul of captured treasure went to the crown.

The Spanish Threat

Ever since his marriage to Mary Tudor, King Philip II of Spain had nurtured dangerous ambitions. As a fervent

Catholic, he hoped to restore the Catholic faith in England. He also dreamed of conquering Elizabeth's troublesome kingdom. During Elizabeth's reign, Spain was increasingly troubled by the English queen and her subjects. In the Netherlands, Elizabeth provided troops and aid in support of the Protestant rebels in their struggle against Spanish rule. On the high seas, English buccaneers, such as Hawkins and Drake, pursued a deliberate policy of attacking and pillaging Spanish ships – with the support and approval of their sovereign.

By 1586, Philip had reached the end of his patience with the English, and he began to make plans for what he called the 'Enterprise of England'. Philip's intention was to send his vast armada of ships to invade England by sea – and it should have been a pushover. While England was a minor player on the world stage, Spain, with its colonies in North Africa and the New World, was a global superpower. But despite her disadvantages, Elizabeth was determined to make the first move. In

1587, with the blessing of his queen, Sir Francis Drake launched a pre-emptive attack on the Spanish port of Cadiz. This bold action, popularly known as the 'singeing of the king of Spain's beard', destroyed ships and supplies intended for the invasion. The sailing of the Armada was delayed for a year, while the English used the time to build up their defences.

Of course, the Armada could not be delayed forever, and on 28 May 1588 the great Spanish fleet set sail from Lisbon under the command of the Duke of Medina Sidonia. The intention was to sail up the English Channel and anchor off Flanders so that an invasion force of 30,000 men could be embarked and landed on English soil. On 19 July, 130 Spanish ships carrying 8,000 seamen and up to 19,000 soldiers entered the Channel. Most of the English fleet was in Plymouth and it numbered less than 100 ships. While they were outnumbered, however, the English ships were well-armed and swift. Their tactics were to avoid close-quarters engagement by standing off, harrying the enemy and bombarding the Spanish with their guns. In a skilful manoeuvre, the English ships slipped behind the Armada, and so got upwind of the Spanish ships – an advantageous position when it came to manoeuvring in combat. For a week the English fleet dogged the tracks of the Armada down the Channel, attacking the Spanish ships whenever they saw an opportunity.

On the night of 28 July as the Armada moored off Calais, the English sent in fireships, vessels packed with inflammable material and gunpowder that were set alight and directed to drift into the Spanish ships. The Spanish panicked and had to cut their anchor cables in order to escape. The following day, the rest of the English fleet attacked the disorganized Spanish formation off Gravelines in a decisive action. However, the English soon ran out of ammunition and withdrew, leaving a westerly wind to drive the Spanish onto treacherous sandbanks. At the last minute, however, the wind changed, allowing the Spanish to escape to the north. They attempted to sail right around the top of Scotland and down the west coast of Ireland to get back to Spain. In the autumn gales, many ships foundered at sea. Others were driven onto the rocks along the Irish coast. Only 60 ships are known to have returned safely to Spain and as many as 15,000 Spaniards perished.

Although the Armada had departed from the Channel, it was not immediately clear that the invasion had been averted. Those on shore braced themselves. Elizabeth herself went to Tilbury in Essex to rally the troops who were mustering to resist any invasion force. Historians offer differing visions of her appearance on this occasion. To some she was a majestic figure clothed in white velvet on a white steed, the sun glinting off her silver breastplate, while Garrett Mattingly's description in his book *Defeat of the Spanish Armada* paints a less flattering portrait of 'a battered, rather scraggy spinster in her middle fifties perched on a fat white horse, her teeth black, her red wig slightly askew, dangling a toy sword and wearing an absurd little piece of parade-armour like something out of a theatrical property-box'.

It is generally agreed that the speech Elizabeth made at Tilbury was truly inspiring (see panel on page 350). And when it became clear that the Armada's destruction had been completed by the weather, the victory seemed to be an act of God. The people of England believed that God was smiling on their Protestant queen, and even her foreign enemies recognized Elizabeth's remarkable nerve in dispelling the mighty power of Spain. King Henry III of France claimed that the English queen's victory 'would compare with the greatest feats of the most illustrious men of past times', while Pope Sixtus was fulsome in his admiration, claiming that 'she certainly is a great queen, and were she only a Catholic she would be our dearly beloved daughter. Just look how she governs! She is only a woman, only mistress of half an island, and yet she makes herself feared by Spain, by France, by the Empire, by all!'

Foreign Wars

The defeat of the Armada was not the end of the conflict

No 'weak and feeble woman'

Elizabeth's speech at Tilbury was addressed to 'My loving people' and emphasized her defiance of all dangers in the certain hope of a glorious victory. In a series of ringing phrases, she stated that:

'I am come amongst you, as you see, at this time, not for my recreation and disport, but being resolved, in the midst and heat of the battle, to live and die amongst you all; to lay down for my God, and for my kingdom, and my people, my honour and my blood, even in the dust.

I know I have the body but of a weak and feeble woman; but I have the heart and stomach of a king, and of a king of England too, and think foul scorn that Parma or Spain, or any prince of Europe, should dare to invade the borders of my realm; to which rather than any dishonour shall grow by me, I myself will take up arms, I myself will be your general, judge, and rewarder of every one of your virtues in the field.

I know already, for your forwardness you have deserved rewards and crowns; and We do assure you in the word

> *of a prince, they shall be duly paid you. In the mean time, my*
> *lieutenant general shall be in my stead, than whom never prince*
> *commanded a more noble or worthy subject; not doubting but by*
> *your obedience to my general, by your concord in the camp, and*
> *your valour in the field, we shall shortly have a famous victory*
> *over those enemies of my God, of my kingdom, and of my people.'*
>
> **Queen Elizabeth I, 9 August 1588, Tilbury**

between England and Spain. While Philip set about repairing his fleet for another invasion attempt, Drake counter-attacked, mopping up some of the Spanish ships that had survived the Armada. In Portugal, the English supported rebels against Philip II and helped to install a pretender on the throne. Then Drake intercepted the annual Spanish treasure fleet coming from the Indies and plunder from the treasure fleets continued to provide significant funds for Elizabeth's exchequer. Three more Spanish armadas set sail for the British waters in 1596, 1597 and 1601. The first two were frustrated again in their endeavours by adverse weather. The 1601 expedition did land Spanish troops in southern Ireland to give assistance to the rebels, but they were eventually defeated and returned home unsuccessful.

Conflict also continued in the Low Countries. After the assassination of William of Orange in 1584, both Queen Elizabeth and Henry III of France declined the offer of sovereignty of the Netherlands. However, under the Treaty of Nonsuch in 1585, Elizabeth accepted the United Provinces as a protectorate and sent out the Earl of Leicester as governor-general with an army of 6,000 men. This turned out to be a very expensive venture, resulting in an annual outlay of £126,180, or around a third of the ordinary expenditure of government.

In France, Elizabeth attempted a difficult balancing act: maintaining cordial relations with the monarchy while offering some support for the Protestant Huguenots in their struggle against the ruling Catholics. However, everything changed in 1589 when King Henry III was assassinated. He was succeeded by Henry IV, who was then a Protestant, and the Catholics rebelled. Elizabeth sanctioned an expedition to Normandy to support the king and Henry finally secured the throne by converting back to Catholicism in 1594.

Elizabeth's foreign wars drained her resources. It is estimated that their cost to the crown was around £4,500,000, while its ordinary revenue was only around £300,000 a year. The queen was forced to sell crown land, raising £800,000, and she also became increasingly dependent on grants from Parliament as her reign advanced. But despite these financial losses, Elizabeth's expenditure on war was very moderate compared with other European monarchs of the time. In her dealing with foreign powers, her first priority was always to ensure the safety and security of her own kingdom, and, unlike her warlike father, she had no wish to build an empire. In 1593, the queen told Parliament, 'My mind was never to invade my neighbours, or to usurp over any. I am contented to reign over mine own, and to rule as a just prince.'

Irish Uprisings

Elizabeth was queen of Ireland as well as England, but the Irish Catholics resented her rule and were more than happy to conspire with England's enemies, especially Spain. Fearing that Ireland could become an invasion base for King Philip II, Elizabeth pursued a policy of making large land grants to her English courtiers. However, the presence of the English aristocracy only exacerbated Irish resentment. In 1559, Shane O'Neill – also known as Shane the Proud – led a revolt against the English in the north-western province of Ulster, even succeeding in crowning himself king of Ulster. Elizabeth temporized over whether she should reach agreement with O'Neill or take arms against him, and the situation was not resolved until 1567 when O'Neill was murdered by members of the rival MacDonnell clan and his lands declared forfeit. In response to this situation, Elizabeth encouraged colonization by English settlers (a policy that became known as 'plantation') in the forlorn hope that their presence would forestall further rebellion.

In 1579, James Fitzmaurice Fitzgerald returned to Ireland from the continent. He had managed to gain papal approval for a Catholic crusade in Ireland, although he lacked material support from France or Spain. When he was ambushed and killed, his cousin Gerald Fitzgerald, Earl of Desmond, took over leadership of the small papal army. However, the uprising proved to be short-lived as English troops brutally suppressed the insurgents. The small force of Italians and Spaniards was massacred, Gerald Fitzgerald was killed and the English government confiscated his lands, burning crops to deprive the local populace of food. The region of Munster in south-western Ireland was devastated and it is estimated that some 30,000 Irish people starved to death. The poet Edmund Spenser wrote that the victims 'were brought to such wretchedness as that any stony heart would have rued the same'.

Between 1594 and 1603, another very significant revolt broke out in Ireland. It was known as Tyrone's Rebellion, or the Nine Years' War, and its leader, Hugh O'Neill, Earl of

Trading Deals

Elizabeth's reign saw the rise of a new merchant class in England and the expansion of international trade. The Muscovy Company was founded in 1555 by Sebastian Cabot. It exported woollen cloth, metals and Mediterranean goods to Russia, bringing back hemp, tallow and rope.

Trading relations were established with the Ottoman Empire. In 1580, a Treaty of Commerce was signed and, the following year, the Levant Company was set up. England exported tin, lead, munitions, cloth, rabbit skins and Spanish silver, receiving in exchange silk, cotton, soft leather, currants, nutmeg, indigo, medicines and soda ash for making glass and soap. During Elizabeth's reign England also began trading with Morocco, exporting armour, ammunition, timber and metals in exchange for sugar.

In 1600, the East India Company was formed to deal in East Indian spices, trade that had been the monopoly of Spain and Portugal until the defeat of the Armada. In the same year, the first Englishman set foot in Japan. William Adams became a counsellor to the Japanese shogun and helped to establish the first commercial treaties between England and Japan.

Tyrone, was backed by Spain. This was a large conflict by the standards of the time – in the early 1600s the English army in Ireland numbered around 18,000 men – and it proved an ongoing problem for Elizabeth's government. In the winter of 1597-8, the French ambassador reported that the Queen 'would wish Ireland drowned in the sea'. The Irish won a significant victory at the Battle of the Yellow Ford in 1598 when around 2,000 English soldiers were killed when their force was ambushed while marching towards Armagh. In 1569, Elizabeth sent her favourite, the Earl of Essex, to put down the revolt. He made little progress militarily and, after a private conversation with O'Neill, he concluded a truce without permission and returned to England. Essex was replaced in Ireland by Charles

Blount, Lord Mountjoy. In 1601 Spanish troops landed in Ireland to support the rebels, but their intervention proved inconclusive and in 1603 Mountjoy finally defeated the rebels. O'Neill surrendered a few days after the death of Elizabeth. The war had been immensely costly and proved a huge drain on England's exchequer.

Elizabeth's People

The growth of the wool trade during the Elizabethan era encouraged the practice of enclosure, as wealthy landowners took over the open land that had traditionally been farmed by the common people. The larger and more profitable farming units formed by the enclosures required fewer people to work on them, forcing peasants to leave the country in the hope of finding work in the towns. At the same time, rising fertility and a falling death rate resulted in a dramatic increase in the English population, which rose from three to four million during Elizabeth's reign. The country's limited resources were stretched to the limit as the population was unable to support itself. On top of this, a number of poor harvests, particularly in the 1590s, resulted in a rise in food prices. Those who could not afford to pay starved and the standard of living dropped for the majority of people. There was a corresponding growth in vagrancy as English towns were plagued by beggars.

In the closing years of Elizabeth's reign a series of Poor Laws were introduced by Parliament to attempt to deal with the problem of widespread poverty. The 1563 Act differentiated between the 'deserving poor', who should be given shelter and alms, and the 'undeserving poor' who should be punished for their vagrancy. It also laid down guidelines for the whipping of able-bodied beggars, who were to be beaten until they reached the parish boundary. Later acts stated that vagabonds should be burned through the right ear and, if they persisted in their profligate ways, they could be imprisoned and even executed.

In 1572, a national poor law tax was introduced to

Elizabethan London

In the Tudor era, London dominated the country (the next two largest towns being Bristol and Norwich), and it grew especially fast under Elizabeth. Between the years 1550 and 1600, its population doubled from 100,000 to 200,000, making it the largest city in Europe. Elizabethan London was a thriving port and commercial centre, renowned for its markets and shops. It was also crowded, dirty, noisy and smelly. Open sewers ran down the middle of the streets and the city was a magnet for thieves, tricksters and beggars who flocked there from across the country.

By Elizabeth's reign, the capital had spread way beyond the limits of its medieval walls. Dominated by the spire of old St Paul's Cathedral and the towers of Westminster Abbey, it had developed into several distinct districts, each with its own character. The great royal palaces were located at Whitehall and Westminster, while nobles' houses lined the Strand, with their gardens sloping down to the river. Each house had its own private jetty, as travelling by barge was much easier than riding through the crowded city streets.

South of the river were the brothels and theatres, including Shakespeare's Globe, while the Tower of London stood on the north bank. The scene of many executions in Tudor times, the Tower also housed the royal menagerie and was a popular visiting place for families. Bear-baiting and cock-fighting were popular public entertainments, and the capital's many inns did a lively trade.

support the needy. It was to be imposed at a local level, collected by the Justice of the Peace and distributed to the 'deserving poor'. Under the 1576 Act, towns were required to provide the unemployed with work in 'poorhouses'. Meanwhile petty criminals, vagrants and beggars were to be confined to 'houses of correction'. In response to the economic crisis and the poor harvests of the 1590s, the famous Poor Law of 1601 required each parish to appoint an overseer to administer relief to the aged and the sick and to poor infants, as well as providing work for the able-bodied in poorhouses (later known as workhouses).

The measures undertaken to counteract poverty in Elizabeth's reign had serious flaws, and workhouses for the poor soon came to be universally feared. However, Elizabeth's Poor Laws marked the first attempt by a government to deal with the problems of the disadvantaged. In a society where the poor could no longer claim the protection of a feudal lord, the Poor Laws represented a very early attempt at a universal welfare system.

A Glittering Court

Elizabeth viewed her royal court as a stage on which she could present a magnificent display. It provided her with the chance to show off the glory and might of the English crown not only to foreign potentates, merchants and ambassadors, but also to her admiring subjects. The Elizabethan court was a moveable spectacle. It could assemble in any of Elizabeth's dozens of royal palaces, or it could take to the road in a stately royal progress, staying at the homes of English nobles.

Typically, the Elizabethan court consisted of around 1,000 people. These included the queen's personal guards and servants, her advisers and a group of courtiers – lords and ladies who gathered around the queen. Musicians and singers, jesters, jugglers and acrobats provided entertainment whenever it was needed. The queen also welcomed companies of actors to perform for her, and extended her royal patronage to especially talented individuals.

The Elizabethan period saw a great flourishing of the arts, actively encouraged by the queen and her courtiers. Portrait painters, such as Nicholas Hilliard and Marcus Gheeraerts, were kept very busy painting the queen and her entourage, and Elizabeth also extended her patronage to musicians, encouraging composers, such as William Byrd and Thomas Tallis, to produce new and adventurous works. Like her father and grandfather, Elizabeth presided over a very musical court. In particular, her chapel choir of men and boys was greatly admired by foreign visitors. One visitor who attended a service in the royal chapel at Greenwich reported, 'In all my travels in France, Italy and Spain, I never heard the like: a concert of music so excellent and sweet as cannot be expressed.'

Poets were always welcome at court. Sir Philip Sidney and Sir Walter Raleigh were accomplished writers of sonnets as well as courtiers, and Elizabeth herself wrote poetry. Edmund Spenser wrote one of the best known poems of the Tudor age as an elaborate compliment to his monarch. *The Faerie Queene* is a verse epic in six books, which describes the adventures of knights, dragons and ladies in distress, but it can also be read as an extended allegory on how to live a life of virtue. At the heart of the poem is Gloriana, the Faerie Queene, a poetic embodiment of Queen Elizabeth.

The art of playwriting took off in Elizabeth's reign with the work of Ben Jonson, Christopher Marlowe and William Shakespeare. The queen was a great lover of dramas and pageants, and many plays had their preview at her court, including Shakespeare's *Twelfth Night* in

Elizabeth's Dresses

Queen Elizabeth is famous for her magnificent wardrobe. She is said to have possessed 3,000 gowns, although many of them were gifts that were never worn. As she grew older, her costumes became increasingly spectacular. Her starched collars and ruffs grew ever larger and, even in old age, she enjoyed wearing very low-cut dresses. Elizabeth's gowns were made from the finest materials – silk, velvet, taffeta, or cloth of gold – and were covered with gems, pearls and gold and silver embroidery. Underneath her gowns, she wore a fine linen shift to protect her dresses (which could never be washed) from perspiration. The queen was also laced into a whalebone corset, and wore a stiff, hooped petticoat, known as a farthingale, which made walking and sitting a challenge. Elizabeth's stockings were made of the finest silk (most of her subjects had woollen stockings) and her royal shoemaker made her a new pair of shoes every week.

1601. There is a story that Elizabeth was so delighted with the character of Falstaff in *Henry V* that she asked

Shakespeare to write a play where Falstaff falls in love. Shakespeare rapidly wrote *The Merry Wives of Windsor* (said to have been composed in just a fortnight) which was much enjoyed by the queen.

Elizabeth's interest in the theatre extended beyond court entertainments. She championed the actors' companies in their struggle against the Puritans who wished to close their playhouses down, and even founded her own acting company, known as the Queen's Men. One of the leading members of the Queen's Men was the comic actor, Richard Tarleton, who could reduce to queen to helpless tears of laughter.

Elizabeth and Essex

When Robert Dudley, Earl of Leicester, died in 1588, he was replaced in the ageing queen's affections by his stepson, Robert Devereux, the Earl of Essex. A handsome and charming courtier, Essex had distinguished himself fighting the Spanish in the Netherlands in 1586, but he was dangerously impulsive and ambitious, prone to forming bitter rivalries and incurring serious debts.

In 1589, Essex disobeyed the queen and joined Drake's expedition to Lisbon – an unsuccessful attempt to drive home the advantage gained by the defeat of the Spanish Armada the previous year. Facing the queen's displeasure when he returned, he soon managed to employ his charms to win her round, and in 1593 he was made a privy councillor, embarking on a long-term struggle for power with William Cecil and his son, Robert.

In 1596, Essex became a national hero when he shared command of the expedition that captured Cadiz from the Spanish. However, the following year, he failed to intercept the Spanish treasure fleet off the Azores. By this time the queen was finding him increasingly unruly. During one row, he turned his back on her (no courtier was ever allowed to turn away from the queen) and she slapped his face. Nevertheless, in 1599, she sent him to Ireland as lord lieutenant. Unable to secure a military victory, he concluded an unfavourable truce, then scuttled back to England to explain himself. Furious that he had dared to disobey her orders, Elizabeth deprived him of his offices and placed him under house arrest.

Essex's response to this humiliation was outright rebellion. He established contact with James VI of Scotland and began to make secret plans to place the Scottish king on the English throne. On 8 February 1601, with several hundred followers, Essex tried to raise a revolt in London, but his rebellion failed to rouse public support. Frightened and humiliated, Essex returned to his home, where he was forced to surrender to Elizabeth's troops. Essex was found guilty of treason and executed on 25 February 1601. Throughout the trial, the queen had been resolute that her former favourite should face execution, but after his death she gave way to depression. For several months she was shaken by fits of weeping, and often withdrew into her darkened bedchamber. In the summer of 1601, she admitted to the French ambassador that she was 'tired of life, for nothing now contented her or gave her any enjoyment'.

The Queen's Last Years

As she entered her late sixties, Elizabeth began to feel her age. Her efforts to maintain a youthful appearance took several hours each morning, and nobody was really deceived by the show she put on. In 1597, the French ambassador reported that the Queen was 'very aged' with a long, thin face under 'a great reddish-coloured wig'. Her teeth were yellow, many of them missing and she could not be understood when she spoke quickly. However, she was still tall and graceful. 'It is a strange thing to see how lively she is in body and mind and nimble in everything she does'. Nevertheless, the embarrassed ambassadors found Elizabeth restless and fidgety, 'for ever twisting and untwisting' her sleeves, and repeatedly opening the front of her robe down to her very navel, as if she were too hot. She also fished for compliments, while complaining that she was 'foolish

Make-up and Wigs

Elizabeth's practice of plastering her face with make-up dated back to her early middle age. Her bout of smallpox, when she was 29 years old, had left her with permanently scarred and pitted cheeks, and – it was reported – partly bald. After her recovery, she adopted a new way of presenting herself to the world. In place of the natural style of her twenties, she wore heavy make-up and a series of elaborate wigs and hairpieces.

Elizabethan ladies commonly applied a 'whitening' lotion to their face and breasts. This compound was often made of ceruse, a mixture of vinegar and white lead, which had the unfortunate side-effect of poisoning the user. Other whitening lotions were made from powdered eggshell, poppy-seeds, borax and alium, while uncooked egg-white was used to 'glaze' the complexion, creating a smooth shell and helping to hide wrinkles. Lips and cheeks were reddened using natural dyes such as madder, cochineal and ochre, but vermilion (mercuric sulphide) was the most popular choice of the fashionable court lady.

Women inserted drops of belladonna in their eyes to make them sparkle, and outlined their eyelids with powdered antimony (a type of kohl powder). Eyebrows were plucked to form a fine, high arch and ladies also plucked hair from their brows to create a fashionably high forehead. Wigs and hairpieces were curled and shaped into elaborate styles and adorned with pearls and other jewels. Wigs were made from human hair, and girls were warned to cover their hair when walking through town at night, in case it should be cut off and turned into a wig.

and old'. The following year, a German visitor said her oblong face was 'fair but wrinkled', her nose hooked and her lips narrow and 'her hair…an auburn colour, but false'.

The queen was also feeling increasingly isolated at court. Following the death of Robert Dudley, the Earl of Leicester, in 1588, she had gradually lost all her most trusted advisers. Sir Francis Walsingham died in 1590, and Sir Christopher Hatton in 1591. Elizabeth's principal adviser William Cecil was also ageing. Although he was deaf and had to be carried everywhere in a chair, he was not allowed to retire because the queen had come to rely on him so heavily. During his last illness, the queen sat by his bed and fed him with a spoon, and she missed him sorely when he finally died in 1598. William was succeeded as chief minister by his son Robert. But Robert Cecil was a colder and more scheming politician than his father and Elizabeth never developed the same close working relationship with him.

While the English people never lost their affection for their monarch, there was a growing feeling of disillusionment in the closing years of Elizabeth's reign. Conflict with Spain had never really ceased, as both sides continued to launch naval attacks on each other, and in an atmosphere of increased suspicion, Elizabeth began to rely more on spies and propaganda. Repression of Catholics intensified and in 1591 the queen authorized special commissions to investigate and question Catholic householders. As Elizabeth's reign advanced, the political system grew more corrupt, with many politicians accepting 'sweeteners' in return for granting special favours. The queen also granted monopolies to favourites as a form of patronage rather than having to depend on Parliament for funds. This led to price-fixing, resulting in resentment among the general public who saw the daily cost of living rising. When Parliament protested, Elizabeth answered her critics with her 'Golden Speech' on 27 October 1601, ending with a resounding statement of her devotion to her people:

'There will never Queen sit in my seat with more zeal to my country, care to my subjects and that will sooner with willingness venture her life for your good and safety than myself. For it is my desire to live nor reign no longer than my life and reign shall be for your good. And though you have had, and may have, many princes more mighty and wise sitting in this seat, yet you never had nor shall have, any that will be more careful and loving.'

Elizabeth's speech won the day. As courtier John Harrington said: 'We all loved her…for she said she loved us.'

The End of an Era

In September 1602, Elizabeth celebrated her 69th birthday. She suffered from rheumatism and her eyesight was failing, but otherwise she seemed to be in good health. Visitors reported that she could still walk briskly and was even capable, on a good day, of riding ten miles on horseback. However, there were signs that her memory was failing and she had begun to find it difficult to concentrate on state affairs.

As the winter advanced, Elizabeth sank into depression, and her sadness was intensified in February 1603 by the death of her close friend Katherine Howard, the Countess of Nottingham. By the beginning of March, she had developed a fever, and was refusing food and unable to sleep. Yet despite her evident weakness, she would not take to her bed nor take any medicines prescribed for her. By 18 March, it was clear that Elizabeth was dying – probably of pneumonia. According to one report, she 'appeared already in a manner insensible, holding her finger continually in her mouth, with her eyes open and fixed to the ground', but it was two more days before she could finally be persuaded to go to bed. From that time on, she ate nothing and began to lose her powers of speech. In the early hours of 24 March 1603, she died peacefully.

Elizabeth's funeral was a grand affair. After five days of lying in state at Richmond Palace (where she had died), the queen's coffin was carried downriver on a barge lit with torches. It was then kept in Westminster Hall until the day of the funeral on 28 April. The coffin arrived at Westminster Abbey on a hearse drawn by four horses wreathed in black velvet and topped by a wax effigy of the queen. Thousands flocked to pay their last tribute to 'Good Queen Bess'. As a contemporary witness wrote 'there was such a general sighing, groaning and weeping as the like hath not been seen or known in the memory of man.'

After Elizabeth

During the queen's final months, Robert Cecil had been busy, secretly preparing the way for a smooth succession. James VI of Scotland had a legitimate claim to the throne as Elizabeth's nearest royal relative, and he was also, importantly, a Protestant. Cecil had encouraged James to humour Elizabeth and his communications had won her approval. It could therefore be assumed that his claim had found favour with her, even though she never named her successor. Consequently, stability was preserved, as the son of Mary, Queen of Scots became the next king of England. King James showed his gratitude for his smooth accession by erecting a magnificent tomb for Elizabeth – along with one for his mother.

Despite the public outpouring of grief at the queen's funeral, many people looked forward to the reign of the new Stuart king. However, in retrospect Elizabeth's reign soon came to be seen as a golden age. For almost 45 years, she had given her country peace and stability. She had strengthened the Church of England, establishing her kingdom as a Protestant country, but one where Catholics could also be tolerated. During Elizabeth's reign, England became an important maritime power and the seeds of international trade were sown. There was also an extraordinary flowering of literature and the arts. More than almost any other monarch, Elizabeth shaped the English identity, instilling a sense of national pride in her people and becoming a living embodiment of the English fighting spirit.

Epilogue:
WHAT WAS THE TUDORS' LEGACY?

The Tudor era lasted for nearly 120 years. From 1485, when Henry Tudor claimed the English throne, to 1603, when Elizabeth I died without an heir, three generations of monarchs presided over an era of enormous change and upheaval. By the time that King James I came to the throne, England had been transformed from a minor medieval kingdom into a major player on the world stage, and the English people had gained a new sense of identity – largely thanks to two charismatic figures: King Henry VIII and his daughter Queen Elizabeth.

The country that Henry VII took over in 1485 was essentially a medieval kingdom. Most of the power rested in the hands of a small group of rival lords, who were often reduced to fighting amongst themselves. A large proportion of the country's land and wealth was owned by the Catholic Church, and the pope expected unquestioning obedience from the English sovereign. English society in the 1480s was in the final stages of feudalism. Trade was mainly conducted with Europe, while the New World was yet to be discovered. On the international front, England was merely a small northern kingdom, threatened by Scotland and France, and its rulers rarely played a significant role in wider politics. But, within a century, all this would change.

By the early 1600s, Elizabeth was ruling over a very different country from the one her grandfather had claimed. The power of the landed aristocracy had been significantly reduced, and the Catholic monasteries had been dissolved. As a consequence of Henry VIII's dramatic quarrel with Rome, England was no longer tied to the Catholic Church, and Elizabeth was head of an independent Anglican Church. After the turbulent reigns of Edward VI and Mary I, religious life in England had settled down. Most people belonged to the Anglican Church, but Catholics were rarely persecuted.

Henry VIII's dissolution of the monasteries had helped to bring about major changes in society, as the vast monastic estates were taken over by secular landowners. At the same time, landowners began to 'enclose' common land, driving peasants away from agriculture and country life and into the towns. By the end of the Tudor period, there were serious problems of poverty and vagrancy in towns, while the monasteries and convents that had once provided a refuge for the poor now no longer existed to fulfil this role. Elizabeth's Poor Laws made some attempt to deal with these acute social problems, but it was left to her successors to face the difficult issue of poverty in towns.

By the 1600s, England was recognized as a significant European power. Henry VIII made an excellent start, building up the English navy and establishing sound coastal defences. Under Elizabeth, England became a formidable sea power, capable of withstanding invasion attempts and of terrorizing foreign ships. While England entered the 17th century with no foreign lands in its possession, having lost Calais during Mary's reign, it was nevertheless regarded as a nation that could command respect and even fear.

At home, the Tudor monarchs established a firm grip over their kingdom, surviving all attempts at rebellion. Even during the troubled reigns of Edward and Mary, the country never descended into anarchy. The Tudors also gradually gained control over more territory. In 1492, Henry VIII achieved the full union of England with the Principality of Wales, while Elizabeth made some progress in asserting her royal authority over Ireland. Scotland remained a threat throughout the Tudor era, but with the succession of James I, union with the Scots was finally achieved.

Under the Tudors, government became more streamlined, as the courts of justice were reformed and taxation was better organized. The Tudor monarchs relied on a few trusted advisers, and Henry VII, Henry VIII and Elizabeth all chose their councillors well. Most of the Tudor monarchs struggled with debt, but Henry VII had laid a firm financial foundation for his dynasty, and Elizabeth made strenuous efforts to maintain control of the royal finances.

The Tudors presided over a period of rapid growth in trade. By the end of Elizabeth's reign, English farmers, manufacturers and merchants had all benefited from a long period of peace and stability. London was flourishing as a centre for international trade and merchants had established valuable trading links with Europe, Asia and the New World. The Tudor monarchs also encouraged building projects, providing the finance for some magnificent palaces, colleges and schools.

Tudor England saw an astonishing flowering of culture. With the active encouragement of the Tudor rulers, drama, poetry, music and art all flourished during the 16th century. The remarkable eruption of talent that overflowed at this time gave the English people a renewed sense of self-confidence and national pride, which was usually focused on their monarch.

All the Tudor kings and queens recognized the importance of display, while Henry VIII and Elizabeth shared a genius for self-presentation. Possibly more than any other monarchs, Henry and Elizabeth managed to inspire a sense of awe and devotion in their subjects. Somehow, these two remarkable but deeply flawed monarchs managed to represent all that was best and noble in the English spirit.

It is a magic that still endures today.